D1288930

rice

from risotto to sushi

rice

from risotto to sushi

Clare Ferguson

photography by Jeremy Hopley

RYLAND
PETERS
& SMALL

Art Director **Jacqui Small**

Art Editor **Penny Stock**

Editor **Elsa Petersen-Schepelern**

Photography **Jeremy Hopley**

Food Stylist **Clare Ferguson**

Stylist **Wei Tang**

Indexer **Hilary Bird**

Production **Kate Mackillop**

**My thanks to Ian Ferguson,
my husband, for his forbearance.**

Notes
Rice is best served immediately after cooking.
If it is to be served cold, or reheated, it should be
cooled quickly after cooking, covered, chilled quickly
in the coldest part of the refrigerator and used within
24 hours.
The herbs in this book are measured in bunches. A
large bunch consists of about 15 stems, and a small
bunch about 5 stems.
Rice has a subtle taste and requires assertive
seasoning with salt, soy sauce, fish sauce or other
salty-tasting agents.

First Published in Great Britain in 1997, reprinted 1997
by Ryland Peters & Small
Cavendish House, 51–55 Mortimer Street, London W1N 7TD

Text © Clare Ferguson 1997
Design and photographs © Ryland Peters & Small 1997

Produced by Mandarin Offset, Hong Kong
Printed in Hong Kong

ISBN 1 900518 12 0

A CIP record for this book is available from the British Library

contents

Of the hundreds of different varieties of rice, some are used only in their country of origin, and others are widely used by cooks all over the world.

rice varieties

Described on pages 140 and 141 are the **different** kinds of rice shown here, together with information about how to cook them and for how long, where to buy them, and how best to use them.

There are **numerous** categories: white, black, red, or brown in **colour**; long, short, medium, or round in **shape**; glutinous (sticky) or not in **texture**; organic or not. Many rice varieties are also available in **easy-cook** form – misleading, because it actually takes longer to cook than ordinary rice. The process was first discovered in ancient India, where parboiling was used to preserve the rice and, in passing, also had the added advantage of forcing some of the nutrients, which are usually destroyed in milling, deep inside the grain.

The result is a food that is much more nutritionally valuable.

Glutinous red rice

White glutinous Japanese sushi rice

Wild rice

White medium grain Calasparra paella rice

Red Camargue wholegrain rice

White basmati rice

Brown basmati rice

Glutinous Thai
fragrant rice

Mixed basmati
and wild rice

Easy-cook
basmati rice

Wholegrain
long grain rice

Brown long grain
easy-cook rice

White round grain
pudding rice

White medium grain
Carnaroli risotto rice

White long grain rice

Long grain white
easy-cook rice

Measuring Rice and Water

The easiest method is by volume: take one container of rice and add multiples of that container of hot water or stock; 1½ times for sushi rice, 2 for most other kinds of rice, 3 for risotto or 4 for paella. Bring to the boil, cover the pan, reduce the heat, simmer until done – usually, though not always, for 12 minutes. This method, translated into grams and millilitres, is used in this book. Alternatively, for boiled rice, cover the rice with liquid to a depth of one finger joint above the rice. Boil, cover, reduce the heat, simmer till done (usually 12 minutes). A Malaysian friend taught me this method when we were students together. It works!

how to cook rice

The best methods for cooking rice range from the most traditional to the most up-to-date and high-tech!

Washing Rice

Asian cooks routinely wash rice before cooking, and sometimes soak it too. I do not believe this is necessary with rice produced by modern farming and milling methods.

Absorption Method

Cover rice with boiling liquid, return to the boil, uncovered. Cover, reduce immediately to the lowest possible heat. Avoid lifting the lid. After 10, 12, 15 or 25 minutes, as listed in the recipes (depending on rice type), it will be cooked and all liquid absorbed. Steam holes may appear on the surface. Turn heat off. Let stand (foil covered, cloth wrapped or not) for a few minutes to allow the grains to fluff up and lighten – or serve straight away.

Pan-of-Water Method

Measure rice into a large pan. Add copious boiling water or stock. Do not cover. Bring back to the boil, reduce to a medium simmer and cook 10, 12, 15, 25 or more minutes, appropriate to the rice type or until tender. Turn off the heat and strain through a sieve. Return rice to the pan, or to a colander set over the still-hot pan. Let stand for a few minutes, then serve and eat.

Electric Rice Cooker

These convenient, fool-proof machines make cooking rice child's play. You should follow the instructions given with each machine, but the usual method is to measure the rice, then add the level of water relevant to that type. Add no salt. Cover and switch on. When rice is done, the machine turns off automatically and the rice will keep hot for up to 1 hour. (After that it will begin to deteriorate.) Perfect for families who eat at different times, though some cooks think this method is somewhat impersonal. Glutinous rice can also be cooked this way, though it takes longer – a microwave is a good alternative.

Cooking Rice in a Microwave

Though no faster than conventional methods it is effortless and useful since the machine automatically turns off and residual heat warms and fluffs up the rice. Choose a large, medium height, non-metal microwaveable casserole or covered bowl. Add 1 scoop (e.g. 300 ml) rice. Measure in 1¾ scoops of liquid for sushi rice, 2 for white or brown rice, 3 for Camargue and Thai red rice, wild rice or risotto rice, and 4 for Calasparra or Bomba rice. Cover. For all kinds of rice, in 750 watt models, microwave on HIGH/100% POWER for 10 minutes or until boiling. For white rice, reduce to MEDIUM/50% POWER for 10–12 minutes. Let stand undisturbed ('cook-on' effect) for 5 minutes. For wild, brown and Camargue red rice, reduce to MEDIUM/50% POWER, cook 30 minutes, let stand 5 minutes. For Thai red rice, reduce to MEDIUM/50% POWER, cook 20 minutes, let stand for 5 minutes. Easy-cook rice of any variety will take 3–4 minutes longer at MEDIUM/50% POWER than the untreated form of that variety. To reheat previously cooked rice, cover and reheat on HIGH/100% POWER for 3–4 minutes (or 6–8 minutes for wild or brown rice.)

Note: *These timings are for an IEC rated 750 watt model. If yours is of higher wattage, deduct 10 seconds per minute of the recipe for every 100 watts. If lower, add 10 seconds per minute of the recipe for each 100 watts.*

Cooking in a Pressure Cooker

Useful for brown rice. Specific instructions should be followed for each model, but this is the general method. Leave the low trivet in position. Add the measured rice. Cover with boiling water or stock. Set lid in position, bring to a gentle simmer, turn the pressure gauge to the higher pressure, reduce the heat, leave to cook. Turn off and remove the pan from the heat. Allow the steam vent to reduce its plume of steam, and let the pan and its contents cool enough to let the pressure reduce. Uncover.

Cooking Rice in the Oven

This is a good but rather slow method. Perhaps the most famous dish cooked in this way is the traditional English rice pudding, where rice, sugar, eggs and milk are cooked in a moderate oven for about 50 minutes.

Steamed Rice

When Asian cooks or restaurants specify 'steamed rice', they may well mean rice cooked in boiling water and steam by the absorption method or even in an electric rice cooker. Traditional South-east Asian recipes for steamed sticky rice may need specific methods relevant to these cultures, where rice cooking is taken to a high art. Follow the recipe instructions, or adapt the method to the utensils you have available.

Sake

(Japanese rice wine)

Pale to deep gold. Sherry, diluted gin or vodka, dry vermouth or Chinese rice wine can be substituted.

Cooking and timing: Use in batters, marinades, dressings, sauces. To serve as a beverage, heat gently over hot water, but do not overheat, or the alcohol will be driven off. Refrigerate any leftover sake after opening.

Mirin

(Japanese sweetened rice wine)

Clear pale yellow liquid, more diluted than sake. If unavailable, substitute as sake.

Cooking and timing: Used in cooked rice, dressings.

Rice Vinegar

(Red, Clear white, Yellow or Black rice vinegar)

Used in dressings, marinades, sauces, dips and rice dishes. Red is mellow, fruity, (almost like balsamic vinegar) with decisive flavour. Clear white is sharp, yellow is mellow, black tastes caramelized. Japanese white rice vinegar is milder than Chinese.

Rice Vermicelli Noodles, Rice Sticks or Wide Rice Sticks

(Vietnamese soup noodles, bañh pho)

Dry, translucent, rice-flour pasta, looped into skeins. Range from very fine vermicelli to wide rice sticks about 1 cm across. Disregard packet cooking instructions which are rarely accurate.

Cooking and timing: Rehydrate in hand-hot or near-boiling water for 5–15 minutes (traditional method is a long soak in cold water). Drain and serve as is, or reheat. Steam-heat, poach, quickly stir-fry, deep-fry, or add to composite dishes.

Vietnamese Ricepaper Wrappers

(Rice wrappers, bañh trang)

Dried 20 or 25 cm ricepaper circles or segments. Eaten raw, steamed or wrapped around fillings, they must first be moistened by dipping in water, or brushing or spraying with water.

Deep-fried, they can also be served as crisps.

Cooking and timing: Soften in hand-hot water, then prepare as above.

other rice products

Ricepaper Wrappers

Wide Rice Sticks

Yellow Rice Vinegar

White Rice Vinegar

Red Rice Vinegar

Rice Sticks

Ricepaper

Japanese *Harusame* Noodles

('Spring Rain' noodles, fine rice noodles)
Dried hair-thin filaments, virtually translucent, made of rice flour (some are also made from potato or tapioca flour). Sold in skeins.
Cooking and timing: As for rice vermicelli noodles.

Mochi Cakes

Hard, dry, dense blocks of pounded, cooked glutinous rice. Not to be confused with fresh mochi cakes which are a ready-to-eat snack.
Cooking and timing: Soften and rehydrate by soaking for about 5–15 minutes in very hot water. Drain then grill or poach. Use in composite dishes such as soups or casseroles.

Ground Rice

Coarse to medium ground meal. Used to make desserts, batters, milk puddings, crisp doughs. Useful thickener, but glutinous rice flour better for fine biscuits, doughs, batters, wrappers.
Cooking and timing: Generally 50 g added to 600 ml of hot liquid. Cooks in about 10–15 minutes.

Rice Flour

Fine flour used for thickening, and to give lightness to sauces, batters and doughs, such as in the steamed buns and *dim sum* of China and South-east Asia. Also used in Asian pasta making. Inexpensive and convenient.
Cooking and timing: Used in doughs, mixtures.

Flaked Rice

Used for puddings, cereals, quick cooking and thickening in hot liquid.
Cooking and timing: 40 g cooked 10–12 minutes in 600 ml hot milk, until thick and creamy.

Rice Crackers

Proprietary snack food, low-calorie, gluten-free. Used with or without toppings as a diet food.

Ricepaper

Made from the fibres of several rice-like plants. Used under baked items to prevent sticking, but is edible, even without cooking. When baking, use moderate oven heat. Brittle when dry.

Ground Rice

Rice Crackers

Harusame Noodles

Mochi Cakes

Flaked Rice

Rice Flour

Rice Vermicelli Noodles

the
americas

Wild rice is the only rice native to North America. However, the many waves of **migration** to the New World has resulted in great, classic rice dishes, that utilize all the other kinds of rice. Dishes range from **gumbo** and **jambalaya** to the creations of modern chefs.

lobster and lemon risotto

on a bed of bitter greens

A superbly luxurious taste of the sea: freshly cooked lobster nestling on lemony risotto and a bed of fresh-tasting salad herbs for contrast. If live lobsters are unappealing or unavailable, buy a recently cooked one and proceed with the recipe the same way, using either ready-made fresh fish stock or fish stock cubes to help boost the flavour of the broth. The dried Japanese-style *wakame* 'sea vegetable' helps add to the sea-savour. Buy *wakame* from a Japanese grocer, specialist deli or wholefood store and use the best risotto rice you can afford. Cheese is an entirely optional addition.

2 tablespoons extra-virgin olive oil

50 g salted butter

2 leeks, white parts only, finely sliced

450 g white Italian risotto rice
(such as *superfino* grade of Carnaroli,
Arborio, Roma or Boldo, or *semifino*
grade of Vialone nano or Padano)

150 ml dry white wine, such as
sauvignon blanc

1.2 litres hot lobster and fish stock
(see method), or fish stock

1 lemon

50 g finely grated Parmesan cheese
(optional)

250 g mixed bitter greens, such as cress,
rocket, mizuna, chicory and
dandelion, to serve

½ teaspoon mild paprika, to serve

Fish Stock:

3 tablespoons sea salt

25 g dried *wakame* seaweed (if available)

1 small, live lobster, about 750 g,
or a ready-cooked lobster

1 teaspoon white peppercorns, crushed

1 head of fennel, quartered,
or 3 celery stalks

12 parsley stalks

500 g bones and trimmings from white
fish such as turbot or cod

Serves 4

To make the fish stock, bring a large pan of water to the boil, together with 3 tablespoons sea salt and the seaweed, if using: there should be enough water to cover the lobster by 5 cm. If using a live lobster plunge it into the boiling water, return to the boil and cook at a rolling boil for 12 minutes, until the lobster turns completely red. Remove the lobster, drain it well, reserving the cooking liquid, and cool over ice for about 10–15 minutes.

Crack open the claws and extract the meat. Cut open the body and tail and remove the edible meat in pieces as large as possible. Discard the inedible parts. Cut the tail meat into thick slices.

Crush the thorax and all the remaining debris and put in a clean pan. Add 750 ml of the strained cooking liquid, 600 ml cold water, the peppercorns, fennel or celery, parsley stalks and the fish bones and trimmings. Bring to the boil, cover, and simmer for about 10 minutes. Strain, taste and adjust the seasoning. Measure 1 litre of this stock into a pan, then reheat and keep hot.

To make the risotto, heat the oil and half the butter in a medium heavy-based saucepan. Add the leeks and fry gently for 1–2 minutes. Add the rice, stir until well coated, then add the wine. Let it bubble.

Add a quarter of the hot stock and stir gently. Cook over a gentle heat for about 6–7 minutes, stirring now and then, until the liquid is absorbed. Continue to add the stock 3–4 times more until it is all used. The risotto should be tender but rich, moist and glossy.

Cut the zest from the lemon into 4 long strips, curl the strips into twists, and set aside. Squeeze the juice from the lemon.

Add the remaining butter to the risotto, followed by lemon juice to taste, and finely grated fresh Parmesan, if using. Stir, cover and allow to heat through.

To serve, put a tangle of salad leaves on each plate and spoon the risotto on top. Put the lobster meat on top of the risotto, sprinkle with paprika, add a twist of lemon zest and serve hot.

pan-fried crab cakes
with spicy oriental sauce

This dish is a blend of several great recipes I first tasted in Louisiana and San Francisco. If no fresh crab meat is available, use defrosted crab. If you have only cooked crab, mix it half and half with raw, minced white fish: it is the dense texture of raw seafood that defines this dish. Season well: the mild sweetness makes salting important.

Put the rice in a medium saucepan with the boiling stock. Return to the boil, cover the pan and reduce the heat to very low. Leave undisturbed for about 18 minutes or until the grains are tender and plump and all the liquid absorbed. Put the pan in a bowl of iced water to cool the rice.

To prepare the crab cakes, finely slice the green tops of the spring onions lengthways. Pour over boiling water, drain and refresh in cold water. Set aside. Chop the white parts finely.

Pick over the crab meat and discard any shell or debris. Put the crab in a food processor together with the chopped white spring onions, ground rice, egg, salt and five-spice. Process in short bursts to amalgamate. (If using cooked crab and raw fish, process these together for a minute or so, in brief bursts, before adding the other ingredients.)

Stir 500 g of cooked rice into the food processor. Process in brief bursts until amalgamated. Do not over-process. Divide the mixture into patties – eight 7 cm diameter as a main course, or eighteen 3.5 cm as a starter.

Heat half the oil in a heavy-based, preferably non-stick frying pan. Cook 4 patties at a time, for 2 minutes each side. Keep hot.

Combine all the sauce ingredients in a small bowl or jug. Mix the spring onion greens into the remaining rice. Serve the rice topped with the crab cakes and the sauce spooned over.

400 g easy-cook basmati wild rice mix

750 ml hot chicken stock

6 spring onions

500 g prepared raw crab meat,
or 175 g cooked crab meat mixed
with 175 g raw minced white fish

25 g ground rice

1 egg

1–2 teaspoons salt

2 teaspoons Chinese five-spice powder

1–2 tablespoons virgin olive oil, for frying

salad greens, to serve (optional)

Spicy Oriental Sauce:

3 tablespoons oyster sauce

3 tablespoons hoisin sauce

1 tablespoon light soy sauce

2 tablespoons sweet ginger wine, or
other dessert wine

1 teaspoon Tabasco sauce

Serves 4 as main course, 6 as starter

red mullet tamales

with tomato chilli dip

Tamales are usually made from corn, but these also contain ground rice. If there is no fresh corn with green husks available, use dried husks from Spanish or Mexican food shops, and rehydrate them in warm water. Chillies, polenta and *masa harina*, the lime-treated cornmeal used in tortillas, are found in the same shops. You can also use frozen green corn husks, and frozen or canned corn 'niblets', mashed a bit with a potato masher. Three corn cobs should yield about 250 g, enough for 6 starters.

375 g fish fillets, such as red mullet, snapper, gurnard, bream or bass
juice of 3–4 limes
1 green jalapeño chilli, finely sliced lengthways
3 fresh corn cobs, including the green husks
125 g rice flour
50 g fine polenta (maize meal)
50 g *masa harina* (limed maize meal)
½ teaspoon chilli powder
1 teaspoon salt
1 tablespoon snipped fresh oregano or marjoram leaves
1 egg, beaten
15 g dried chilli, such as ancho or chipotle, crumbled or chopped
3 ripe red tomatoes, finely diced
salt, to taste
Serves 6 as a starter

tamales de pescado

1 Cut the fish into 24 equal pieces and put them into a non-reactive dish. Add the lime juice and the jalapeño chilli. Stir well and set aside to marinate while the tamale dough is prepared.

2 Remove the green husks from the corn and put them in a bowl of hot water. Discard the silk. Using a coarse grater, grate the fresh corn to a pulp. Discard the central cores. (There should be about 250 g of pulp.)

3 Mix the pulp with the rice flour, polenta, *masa harina*, chilli powder, salt and herbs. Add the beaten egg and 2–3 tablespoons of fish marinade. Mix to a soft, pliable, putty-like dough. Drain the fish and reserve the marinade.

4 Drain the husks. Put a piece of fish at the end of a husk, with a heaped tablespoon of dough on top. Wrap up loosely, over and over, until half enclosed. With a second husk, wrap at right angles. Secure with string or skewer.

5 Repeat with all the remaining tamales. Steam over rapidly boiling water for 15–20 minutes, turning the parcels after 10 minutes. Test by unwrapping: the fish should be white and the dough firm.

6 Simmer the reserved marinade for 4 minutes, then add the crumbled dried chilli. Add the diced tomato and stir. Serve with the tamales.

Note: If you don't have enough corn husks, use oiled foil strips instead.

jambalaya

traditional jambalaya
with chorizo and prawns

The word 'jambalaya' is Louisiana Creole: *jam* is from *jambon*, the French word for ham, *à la* means 'of' or 'with', and *ya* is an old African word for rice. Jambalaya relates to Senegalese *tiebe* dishes, Caribbean pilaus and Spanish paella. It includes the Southern culinary 'trinity' of celery, green pepper and onion, and the browned roux of butter and flour, a pivotal element in Southern cooking.

Heat the oil in a large, heavy-based, flameproof casserole. Stir in the flour, if using, and cook to a golden-brown roux. Add the pork and sausage and cook, stirring and turning, for 6–7 minutes until brown. Remove from the pan using a slotted spoon. Add the chicken and sauté until golden-brown and firm. Return the pork and sausage to the pan, add the celery, onion, garlic, pepper or chillies, bouquet garni and chilli flakes. Stir for 2 minutes more. Add the tomatoes and rice, and stir until the rice is well coated. Add the hot stock, return to the boil, cover and reduce to a gentle simmer. Cook undisturbed for 10–12 minutes, then add the ham and prawns. Cover and cook for another 4–5 minutes until the prawns are pink and firm, the ham hot, the liquid almost completely absorbed, and the chunks of meat plump and tender. Stir gently. Cover the pan and stand for 3–4 minutes with the heat turned off. Serve from the casserole.

3 tablespoons corn or canola oil
2 tablespoons plain flour (optional)
375 g pork shoulder, boneless pork chops or fillet, cut into 2.5 cm chunks
375 g spicy pork link sausage, (chorizo or *andouille*), cut into 2.5 cm chunks
8 boneless, skinless chicken thighs
2 celery stalks, sliced
I large onion, sliced
4 garlic cloves, crushed
I green pepper, deseeded, cored and diced, or 2 deseeded jalapeño chillies
I bouquet garni (a bundle of fresh bay, thyme, parsley and sage, tied together)
I teaspoon dried chilli flakes
500 g ripe fleshy red tomatoes, chopped
500 g white long grain rice
I litre boiling chicken or pork stock
125 g smoked ham, in long slices
250 g uncooked prawn tails, shell-on
salt and freshly ground black pepper
Serves 4–6

cajun gumbo
with Jerusalem artichokes

Gumbo has an intriguing and exotic past with French, Spanish and African heritage. It evolved out of necessity but it has been elevated to the glorious. *Gombo* is French for 'okra', and traditionally okra is trimmed to show its interior and oozes sticky juices which enrich the texture of the dish. I prefer to trim just a little from the stem end, without exposing the interior, so it cooks tender but firm. Filé powder, a traditional thickener and flavouring made from sassafras trees, is available from specialist shops.

2 tablespoons fruity olive oil
250 g chorizo, Cajun or Creole spicy sausage, or boudin, cut in chunks
6 chicken thighs
2 onions, quartered
4 celery stalks, with leaves reserved, then scissor-snipped
2 green peppers, deseeded and cubed
1 big bunch of fresh thyme
2 hot chillies, such as jalapeño or serrano, deseeded and chopped
1 teaspoon allspice berries, crushed
2 teaspoons white peppercorns, crushed
250 g Jerusalem artichokes, scrubbed and thinly sliced
600 ml spicy stock, such as pork
2 tablespoons filé powder (or extra thyme leaves plus 2 tablespoons arrowroot for thickening)
about 400 g canned chilli beans, in their sauce
1–2 teaspoons Tabasco sauce
250 g white easy-cook long grain rice, such as Carolina
125 g okra, tops minimally trimmed
2 plum tomatoes, cubed
Serves 4–6

1 Heat the olive oil in a large, heavy-based flameproof pan. Add the thick chunks of spicy sausage, the chicken thighs and the quartered onions, then sauté for 6–8 minutes until lightly browned.

2 Thickly slice the celery stalks (but not the leaves) and add to the pan together with the green pepper, thyme, chilli, crushed allspice berries and pepper. Sauté for a further 5 minutes.

3 Add the thinly sliced artichokes, together with the hot spicy stock, then return to the boil, cover the pan with a lid, reduce the heat and simmer gently for another 20 minutes. Mix the filé powder with a little water.

4 Stir in the chilli beans and their sauce, Tabasco to taste, and the green filé mixture. Heat through and thicken slightly. Wash and drain the rice and put in a shallow saucepan. Add double its volume of boiling water.

5 Bring the rice back to the boil, cover, reduce the heat and simmer for about 15 minutes. Add the trimmed okra after 8 minutes: it will cook in the steam. Leave to stand 3 minutes.

6 Serve the gumbo with the rice, in generous bowls, garnished with the reserved celery leaves and diced tomato. Alternatively, serve the gumbo first, then serve the rice afterwards, to stir into the juicy gravy.

Modern Florida cooking is very adventurous: passionfruit and lime are used to marinate the fish, and then added to the dressing. Wild rice is native to America, and makes a delicious, modern salsa when mixed with black beans and the spicy, fruity marinade.

seared swordfish
with wild rice and black bean salsa

4 swordfish steaks, about 175 g each, cut about 1 cm thick

6 garlic cloves, cut into 5 or 6 slivers

salt and freshly ground black pepper

Black Bean Salsa:

175 g dried small black soybeans, turtle beans or kidney beans

(or 450 g canned black kidney beans)

1 onion, quartered

1 bouquet garni or bunch of thyme

175 g wild rice

Passionfruit and Lime Marinade:

6 tablespoons chopped fresh coriander

2 spring onions, chopped

2 hot chillies, deseeded and chopped

1 teaspoon sea salt

pulp or juice of 6 passionfruit

1 teaspoon cumin seeds, crushed

2 red peppers, deseeded and diced

150 ml extra-virgin olive oil

1 teaspoon peppercorns, crushed

juice of 6 limes

Serves 4–6

To make the salsa, first soak the dried beans overnight in cold water to cover. Next day, drain the soaked beans and enough boiling water to cover the beans by 7 cm. Add the onion and bouquet garni. Bring to the boil, then simmer part-covered for 1¼–1½ hours until the beans are soft enough to squash easily between the fingers. After 45 minutes, put the wild rice in a pan with 900 ml boiling water. Return to the boil, cover and simmer for 40–45 minutes until the grains are tender and some are splitting at the ends. Let stand for about 10 minutes, then drain.

Make 8 cuts in each fish steak, 4 on each side, and insert slivers of garlic. To make the marinade, mix the salt, passionfruit, cumin, red pepper, oil, pepper and half the lime juice. Whisk briefly. When the rice is half cooked, pour the mixture over the fish and set aside to marinate for 20 minutes. Reserve about 6 tablespoons of the beans and put the remainder in a bowl with the rice.

Boil the marinade in a pan for 1 minute. Add the remaining lime juice. Pour half this mixture into a bowl, and stir the remainder through the rice and beans.

To finish the salsa, add the coriander, spring onions, chillies and reserved beans to the bowl of marinade. Season generously. Season the fish, then cook on a preheated grill, barbecue or stove-top grill pan for 2½–3 minutes: no longer or it will dry out. Set the fish on the rice-bean base, add the salsa and serve hot, warm or cool, but not chilled.

rice and peas
with Jamaican hot chilli sauce

Peas or beans with rice is one of the world's greatest food combinations. Depending on the culture and location, 'peas' could mean pigeon peas, black-eyed peas, gunga, gungo, goongo or Congo peas, red beans, black beans or even fava beans. Refer to a specialist cookbook for the different soaking and cooking times needed for each variety – kidney beans, for example, must be thoroughly boiled to eliminate toxins. In this recipe, the hot Caribbean chillies are left whole but pierced, to provide fruitiness as well as heat.

500 g dried peas or beans, such as pigeon peas, gungo, black-eyed peas, red or black kidney beans, or black turtle beans*

2 habanero or Scotch bonnet chillies, pierced several times with a needle

1 onion, quartered

750 g smoked shoulder bacon or ham, or 1 bacon or ham hock

500 g white long-grain rice, or white easy-cook rice

400 ml canned coconut milk

Chilli Sauce:

4 garlic cloves, crushed

2 medium hot green chillies, such as serrano or jalapeño, deseeded and chopped

1 bunch fresh oregano, snipped

1 bunch fresh flat leaf parsley, scissor-snipped

8 spring onions, chopped

juice of 5 limes or 3 lemons

1 tablespoon mixed French mustard

salt, to taste

Serves 6–8

*Dried peas or beans should be soaked overnight, then cooked, according to their variety, as described in Step 6.

1 To soak the peas or beans, cover with cold water and leave overnight, or pour over boiling water, cover with a lid and soak for 1 hour. Drain. If using red beans, boil vigorously for 15 minutes, then discard the water.

2 Put the beans in a pan with boiling water to cover by 7 cm. Add the chillies, onion and bacon, ham or pork. Boil for 10 minutes, part-cover and cook at a moderate boil according to the times in Step 6, or until fairly tender.

3 Add the rice and coconut milk. Simmer, part-covered, for 16–18 minutes. Drain off any liquid into a pan, reduce to 2 tablespoons and return to the beans. Discard the chillies. Remove the meat, slice, then return to the pan.

4 To make the chilli sauce, crush the garlic, deseed and slice the chillies, and snip the herbs. Put with the other sauce ingredients in a food processor. Whizz for the minimum time it takes to form a sauce.

5 Carefully remove the cooked habanero or Scotch bonnet chillies from the pan, and discard. Serve the rice and peas in bowls with a dollop of chilli sauce on top, and serve the remaining sauce separately.

6 Cooking times for presoaked peas or beans are 40–50 minutes for red* or black kidney beans, 1¼–1½ hours for black-eyed and gungo peas, 1½–2 hours for black turtle beans.

Many European rice dishes are a legacy of the continent's **colonial** past, especially **kedgeree**, Britain's favourite dish from the great days of the Raj. Spain and Italy, however, have created their own classic rice dishes, **paella** and **risotto**, using local strains of rice.

europe

Kedgeree, that remnant of Britain's Indian colonial past, depends on first class ingredients and recently cooked, cool (not chilled, not hot) rice for its full charm. Though traditionally a breakfast dish, it is perfect for brunch, lunch or a late, informal supper meal. If you have other smoked seafood such as scallops, mussels, oysters, or even clams, these too may be added to the poaching water to reheat before mixing with the rice. Versatile, elegant, easy and utterly delicious, especially when accompanied by a cold, crisp sauvignon blanc or champagne.

kedgeree
with smoked fish and crème fraîche

500 g smoked haddock
50 g unsalted butter
2 red onions, finely sliced
3–4 garlic cloves, chopped
I teaspoon coriander seeds, crushed
I pinch of turmeric or saffron
250 g cooked white basmati rice
2 soft-boiled (4 minutes) eggs
100 ml crème fraîche
I medium hot red chilli, deseeded,
blanched and finely sliced (optional)
sea salt and freshly ground pepper
sprigs of parsley, to serve
Serves 4

Poach the fish in a little water for 4–6 minutes until it flakes easily. Discard the skin, remove any bones, break the fish into chunky pieces, then return it to its still-hot cooking liquid. If you plan to use any other cooked seafood, add it to the cooking liquid at this time.

Heat the butter in a pan and add the onions, garlic, coriander seeds and turmeric or saffron, and sauté for 2 minutes. Add the drained, flaked fish, the cooked rice, 1–2 tablespoons of poaching liquid, and the eggs, shelled and cut into quarters. Cover the pan and reheat for 2 minutes. Stir in the salt and freshly ground black pepper, the crème fraîche and sliced red chilli, if using.

Pile into a serving dish, add sprigs of parsley and serve hot. Triangles of fresh hot toast make a pleasant accompaniment.

Suppli are rice balls, cooked to pleasing crispness outside, melted and gooey inside. The dribbly melted mozzarella cheese oozes strings or 'wires', the origin of their charming Italian name. Use risotto left over from an earlier meal – cook extra because *suppli* are so delicious – or other cooked round grain rice. The key thing is to ensure that the rice, at the outset, is flavourful: under-seasoned *suppli* are disappointing.

supplì al telefono

suppli cheese balls
with basil and pine nuts

50 g pine nuts

1 kg seasoned, cooked risotto rice

2 medium eggs, beaten

1 bunch of basil, finely sliced

75 g Parma ham, thinly sliced, cut into 36 squares

125 g buffalo mozzarella cheese, cut into 36 little strips

125 g dry breadcrumbs

olive oil, for frying

Makes about 36, serves 6–8

Preheat the grill, line the grill pan with foil and toast the pine nuts, shaking them occasionally under the heat until they are evenly golden brown. Fold these into the rice, together with the eggs and basil. Mix well.

Shape, using clean hands, into about 36 walnut-sized balls. Use your index finger to push a hole into the centre of each. Insert a piece of ham, followed by a piece of mozzarella. Pinch closed and squeeze the ball back into shape.

Roll each croquette in breadcrumbs, then chill.

Heat the oil in a deep-fryer or saucepan to 190°C or until a cube of bread turns golden brown in 40 seconds. Using a frying basket, cook several at a time, rolling them around and turning them over with tongs, so that the *suppli* are evenly golden brown all over (about 3 minutes). Ensure there is enough oil to cover the *suppli*, or they may split during cooking because of uneven expansion.

Drain on crumpled kitchen paper and keep hot until all the *suppli* are cooked. Serve hot as a starter, or as party food.

caldo verde soup

A classic Portuguese soup – hot, spicy and outstandingly delicious. It depends upon fresh greens, good broth, garlic, chilli, potatoes and, in this version, rice too. A marvellously adaptable recipe that varies from this thick, hearty form to clear broths with a few shreds of potato and greens.

Heat the oil or fat in a large heavy-based pan, add the onions, garlic, chilli, rice and potatoes, and sauté for 2–3 minutes. Chop the parsley and coriander and reserve half of each. Add the remainder to the pan, followed by the cabbage and the greens. Pour in the pork stock and season to taste. Bring the soup to the boil, cover and simmer for about 20–25 minutes, or until pulpy and tender. Strain through a colander or sieve, reserving the liquid and solids but discarding the chilli. Put the reserved parsley and coriander in a blender or food processor, add about one-third of the liquid and solids and blend to a purée. Return the purée and the remaining soup to the pan and return to the boil. Taste and adjust the seasoning.

Meanwhile if using bacon, cut it into lardons (matchstick strips) or, if using pancetta, cut it into cubes. Put the lardons or cubes into a small pan and sauté in their own fat until crisp. Pour the pan contents into the soup. Heat the caraway seeds in a second pan until aromatic, sprinkle over the soup and serve, accompanied by some crusty country bread.

3 tablespoons good virgin olive oil, lard or bacon fat

2 onions, quartered and sliced

4 garlic cloves, crushed

1 hot green chilli, such as serrano, slit open lengthways

125 g long grain rice

175 g potatoes, cut in 1 cm cubes

1 large bunch of fresh flat leaf parsley

2 large bunches of fresh coriander

250 g dark green cabbage, such as Savoy

125 g Swiss chard, spinach, beet greens or broccoli tops

1.5 litres flavourful pork stock

50 g bacon or pancetta

1–2 teaspoons caraway seeds

sea salt and freshly ground black pepper

Serves 4–6

A glorious, sunshine-coloured Provençal soup, using the dry, brilliantly orange-fleshed pumpkin (*calabaza*, in West Indian markets), with its dark, heavy rind, firm flesh, and hard seeds. You could substitute a firm, dense squash, such as Hubbard or butternut, but not watery summer squash.

soupe de potiron

pumpkin chowder
with rice and thyme

1.5 kg orange-fleshed pumpkin, peeled and deseeded (about I kg)
I large Spanish onion, sliced
600 ml well seasoned chicken stock
I teaspoon dried crushed chillies
I½ teaspoons salt
I cinnamon stick, broken
I small bunch of thyme, plus extra to serve
I fresh bay leaf, bruised
100 g white long grain rice
300 ml full-cream milk
Serves 6

Cube the pumpkin and put in a pan with the onion, stock, chillies, salt, cinnamon, thyme and bay leaf. Bring to the boil, cover, and cook for 20 minutes or until done. Meanwhile, put the rice in another pan with boiling water to cover by 2.5 cm. Bring to the boil, cover, reduce the heat, and simmer for 15 minutes until most of the water has been absorbed. When the vegetables are soft and pulpy, remove and discard the bay leaf and thyme. Reserve the cinnamon.

Using a blender, purée the soup in batches to a creamy consistency. (A food processor will give a less silky texture.) Add the drained rice and milk, then taste and adjust the seasonings. Bring to the boil, simmer for 5 minutes, and serve with thyme sprinkled over the top, and a few reserved shards of the cinnamon, if preferred.

Note: This chowder may be served chilled, with hot garlic or herb bread, or *fougasse*, the lacy Provençal bread.

Buckwheat flour, even in Russia, is usually combined with plain flour for best results. Rice flour is used here instead, giving some tenderness and a mild sweetness to balance the nutty buckwheat taste. This recipe adds the eggs all at once, rather than separating them, and so is quicker and easier.

rice and buckwheat blini

100 g rice flour
100 g buckwheat flour
2 teaspoons micronized yeast,
or a 15 g sachet
450 ml milk
2 tablespoons extra-virgin olive oil
1 tablespoon clear honey
1 teaspoon sea salt flakes
1 egg
6–8 tablespoons olive oil, lard or
clarified butter, for frying
Toppings:
a choice of: melted butter and
soured cream; crème fraîche (about
50 g per person), plus 1 tablespoon
scissor-snipped chives; beluga caviar
or keta (salmon roe); smoked trout,
salmon, halibut or sturgeon; pickled
herring (about 50 g per person)
Makes about 48,
serves 6 as a starter,
or 8 as party food

Sift the flours with the powdered yeast. Bring the milk to blood heat (a drop on the inside wrist feels barely warm), by heating in a saucepan, or microwaving on HIGH/FULL for about 1½ minutes. Add the oil, honey and salt, and stir.

Pour this liquid all at once into the dry ingredients. Whisk to form a batter the consistency of thick cream. Stand the batter in a warm place for 20–40 minutes (or longer if you have the time), or until a few bubbles appear. Whisk in the egg. Heat one (or two) pancake griddles or heavy-based frying pans. Add a little oil, lard or clarified butter. Spoon in 4 pancakes at a time (each about 1 tablespoon). Cook over moderate heat for about 1 minute until bubbles form all around the edges. Flip the pancakes over and cook for a further minute, or until firm and golden. Keep them warm until all are made.

Serve with a selection of the suggested toppings, such as the crème fraîche and chives, and the soured cream and caviar shown here – and a glass of iced vodka.

Note: To speed the cooking process, use two frying pans – this way, the blini are done in under 15 minutes and remain velvety and fresh.

This vegetarian version of the classic dish came from a *kafenion* on the Ionian island of Zante where dried fruits are a major crop. Serve these as a starter – as part of a mixed *meze* with feta, olives and pickled chillies, for example – and always with a bowl of authentic, thick Greek plain yoghurt. A glass of ouzo is an extra treat.

greek dolmathes

250 g fresh vine leaves, or preserved vine leaves, drained (about 50–60)

250 g onions, quartered and finely sliced

125 g spring onions or baby leeks, trimmed and finely sliced

1 large bunch of fresh herbs, such as parsley, mint and/or dill, chopped

150 ml extra-virgin olive oil

150 g long grain white rice, soaked briefly in cold water

50 g currants

25 g pine nuts

2 lemons

600–750 ml boiling vegetable stock

2 teaspoons salt

freshly ground black pepper

To Serve:

1 tub Greek yoghurt, about 250 ml

2 lemons, cut into wedges

Makes about 45–55, serves 6–8

If using brine-preserved leaves, leave them in a colander under running cold water until the sink is half full. Agitate them, then leave to drain. If using fresh leaves, blanch 5–6 at a time for about 1 minute in a large pan of boiling salted water. Rinse in cold water and drain in a colander.

Mix the onions and spring onions or leeks with the herbs, half the oil and the drained rice. Season to taste. Stir in the currants, nuts and the juice of 1 lemon. Put 1 heaped teaspoon of filling at the stalk end of each leaf. Roll this end then the two side flaps over towards the centre, neatly but not too tightly. Roll up, keeping the seam beneath, leaving room for expansion. Continue until all the filling has been used.

Put half the remaining leaves over the base of a large pan, flameproof casserole or frying pan, overlapping each leaf. Pack in the dolmathes in concentric circles. Cover with the remaining leaves and a flat, heatproof plate.

Pour in boiling stock until just covered, add the salt, then bring to the boil, cover, reduce the heat and simmer for about 45–55 minutes or until rice is sticky, swollen and tender. Leave to stand undisturbed for 10 minutes. Drain if necessary. Serve hot or warm, but not chilled. Drizzle with the remaining oil and serve with yoghurt and lemon wedges.

paella valenciana
spanish paella
with chicken, prawns and squid

Spain's paella is a handsome, one-pan dish. Use a round, short grain Spanish paella rice such as Bomba, or the famous Calasparra, from Spanish grocers, or an Italian risotto-style rice. Allow two handfuls, or 75–100 g per person for paella, and cook for about 18 minutes (or 25–30 for Calasparra, which may also need more water). The fiercer heat, the lack of stirring and the fact that the rice goes directly into the boiling liquid all make this very different from a risotto.

8 small squid

1 kg live mussels, scrubbed

150 ml white wine

6 tablespoons extra-virgin olive oil

500 g chicken cut into chunks

750 g chorizo, cut into chunks

16 uncooked medium prawns, shell-on, heads removed and reserved for stock (see below)

8 uncooked langoustines

1 large Spanish onion, sliced

2 red peppers, deseeded and sliced

1 whole garlic head, trimmed

2 large fleshy tomatoes, chopped

2 teaspoons sweet paprika

500 g paella rice or risotto rice

250 g podded, skinned broad beans

1 pinch of saffron threads

6 tablespoons scissor-snipped fresh flat leaf parsley, to serve (optional)

Fish Stock:

prawn heads (see above)

1 kg white fish bones or heads

1 large bouquet garni (sprigs of thyme, bay, flat leaf parsley, celery and orange zest, tied together)

2 teaspoons black peppercorns

1 Spanish onion, quartered

2 carrots quartered

300 ml medium white wine

1.5 litres cold water

1–2 teaspoons sea salt

Serves 8

1 To make the stock, put all the ingredients, except the salt, in a pan, bring to the boil, and simmer for 10–15 minutes. Skim several times. Strain back into the rinsed pan, and continue simmering for 15–20 minutes. Add seasoning.

2 To prepare the squid, gently pull apart the head and body. Cut off and reserve the tentacles from the head section. Remove and discard the plastic-like stiffener and soft roe from the body. Remove the skin if preferred.

3 Discard any open or heavy mussels. Put in a pan with the white wine. Boil fiercely, covered, until they open (about 1–2 minutes). Remove them one by one and set aside. Strain the liquid into the stock, producing 1.5 litres.

4 Heat half the oil in a large paella pan or frying pan. Add the prawns, langoustines and squid and fry briefly until barely set. Remove and set aside. Add the chicken and chorizo, and brown over moderate heat for 10–12 minutes.

5 Add the onion, pepper, garlic, tomatoes, stock and half the paprika. Bring to a rapid boil, stir in the rice, reduce the heat to a gentle simmer and cook, uncovered, without stirring, for 16–18 minutes or until the rice is cooked.

6 Add the beans, saffron, remaining paprika and oil. Stir, add all the seafood, then cook for 8–10 minutes on a very low heat until the rice is fully cooked and dry. Add extra stock or water as necessary. Serve, sprinkled with parsley.

Italian risotto is remarkably straightforward if quality ingredients are used. Fresh butter, best risotto rice such as Carnaroli or Arborio, a glass of good wine and strong, flavourful stock are all essentials.

risotto alla milanese

saffron risotto

75 g salted butter

I medium onion, sliced

3–4 garlic cloves, crushed (optional)

450 g white Italian risotto rice

125 ml white wine

I large pinch of saffron threads

¼ teaspoon sea salt flakes

(or, if stock is salty, sugar)

I litre boiling chicken stock

75 g fresh Parmesan cheese (or *grana padano*), finely sliced

freshly ground black pepper

sprigs of flat leaf parsley, to serve

Variation – Wild Mushroom Risotto:

25 g dried porcini mushrooms, broken

15 g dried morel mushrooms, broken

I litre boiling chicken stock

125 ml robust red wine

flat leaf parsley, to serve

(omit the saffron and salt)

Serves 4

Heat 50 g of the butter in a medium-sized, heavy-based saucepan. Add the onion and garlic, if using, fry gently for I minute, then stir in the rice and the wine. Let it bubble away. Grind the saffron, salt or sugar in a small bowl, then add a ladle of stock. Pour half this mixture into the rice and reserve the remainder. Continue simmering the rice, adding ladles of boiling stock at intervals, until all the liquid is used and absorbed (about 28 minutes). The risotto should be tender but still very rich, moist and glossy. Alternatively, add all the stock at once and cook over a low heat for 28–32 minutes, stirring gently from time to time.

Add the remaining butter and saffron, then stir in half the cheese and some pepper. To serve, sprinkle with the remaining cheese and garnish with sprigs of parsley.

For the mushroom variation, put the mushrooms in a pan and add the hot stock. Simmer, covered, for 10–15 minutes, until dark and flavourful. Strain and reserve the liquid. Rinse the mushroom pieces. Proceed as for saffron risotto but omit the saffron and salt or sugar, and use red wine instead of white. The rinsed mushrooms should be cooked with the rice. Though purists would omit the cheese, I always include it.

spicy camargue rice
with char-grilled duck breasts

Red rice from the Camargue in the South of France is a rogue strain with a pretty red-brown colour. A wholegrain rice, chewy and interesting, it seems destined to become a new and fashionable ingredient. Similar red rice strains also grow in other areas, such as India and the American South.

Rub the duck with the garlic, snipped tarragon, honey and peppercorns. Marinate in a non-reactive dish for 15 minutes.

Put the rice in a medium, heavy-based pan, cover with the stock, return to the boil, cover and simmer for 30 minutes. To make the onion confit, put the sliced and blanched onions in a pan with the jelly and vinegar, and stir until the jelly has dissolved and a glaze forms. Set aside.

Oil and preheat a cast-iron stove-stop grill pan or char-grill. When the rice is almost cooked and stock almost completely absorbed, set the four *magrets*, skin sides down, on the grill. Drizzle over the remaining oil. Cook, pressing down firmly with a fish slice or spatula, for 8–10 minutes altogether. The duck surface should be seared and part-caramelized but the centre, when pushed with a finger, should still feel semi-soft: it should remain rosy yet be well warmed through.

Put the cooked duck breasts on top of the cooked rice and pour over the remaining marinade. Cover the pan again and cook for a further 10 minutes over low heat. Remove the *magrets* and set them aside to rest. Stir most of the onion confit into the rice (drained, if necessary).

To serve, spoon the rice on to heated dinner plates. Slice the duck breasts and arrange on top of the rice, add generous spoonfuls of very cold crème fraîche, a sprig of tarragon and a trickle of the onion confit, then serve.

4 *magrets de canard* (**Barbary duck breast portions**), **about 1 kg total**

4 garlic cloves, crushed

4 sprigs of French tarragon, scissor-snipped, and 4 sprigs, to serve

2 tablespoons clear, scented honey

2 teaspoons green peppercorns, crushed

2 tablespoons extra-virgin olive oil

8 tablespoons crème fraîche, to serve

Spicy Red Camargue Rice:

400 g red Camargue long grain rice (or American red rice)

750 ml boiling duck, chicken or pork stock

Onion Confit:

2 red onions, thinly sliced, blanched briefly in boiling water and dried

4 tablespoons redcurrant, gooseberry or guava jelly

2 tablespoons red wine vinegar

Serves 4

This Byzantine-style rich rice stuffing for my Christmas turkey was taught to me by an Athenian political journalist and epicure. It works equally well with other kinds of poultry, feathered game and larger whole birds (add to the roasting tin 35–40 minutes before the end of the cooking time).

chestnut rice stuffing
with roasted turkey breast

1.25 kg turkey breast joint

extra-virgin olive oil

4 tablespoons Greek ouzo (or raki)

salt and freshly ground black pepper

Chestnut Rice Stuffing:

2 onions, chopped

4 garlic cloves, chopped

100 g dried apricots or figs

50 g walnut halves

50 g salted, roast almonds

1 small orange

8 tablespoons extra-virgin olive oil

250 g white long grain rice

100 g seedless raisins

375 g prepared cooked, unsweetened shelled chestnuts

25 g pine nuts

1 teaspoon allspice berries, crushed

2 teaspoons ground cinnamon

2 teaspoons dried oregano

1 large bunch of flat leaf parsley, scissor-snipped

750 ml chicken or turkey stock

Serves 6–8

Rub the turkey with oil, salt and pepper and put in a roasting tin. Roast, uncovered, in a preheated oven, at 190°C (375°F) Gas Mark 5. Allow 20 minutes per 500 g and 20 minutes extra – about 70 minutes in total.

To make the stuffing, first chop the dried fruit, walnuts, almonds and the orange, including the skin and pith. Heat the oil in a heavy-based pan, and sauté the onions, garlic and rice for 2 minutes, then add the all the stuffing ingredients. Return to the boil, cover and simmer for 8 minutes or until the rice is par-cooked and much of the liquid absorbed. (The turkey should have been cooking for about 40 minutes.)

Pour the rice stuffing and its liquid around the turkey. Pour over the ouzo. Cover the tin with a double layer of foil, pinching tightly closed all around the edges, or with a tight-fitting lid. Return to the oven for 30–35 minutes.

Uncover the pan and test the turkey for doneness: the juices should run clear and gold, without a trace of pink, when the fleshiest part of the breast is pierced with a knife. (Catch the juices in a metal spoon to show the colour.) Leave the turkey and its stuffing, covered, to stand in a warm place for 5 minutes, to develop maximum succulence. Carve in large, even slices. Serve with a mound of the stuffing, either immediately while hot, or chilled the next day. Crisp cos lettuce hearts and a yoghurt-based dressing make excellent accompaniments.

kohlrouladen

stuffed cabbage leaves
with sauerkraut and a red pepper sauce

Traditionally, this hearty, oven-baked dish might be served with tomato sauce and green peppers. This version uses canned red peppers, roasted and skinned, often labelled 'pimiento'. Both colour and flavour remain bright and clear. You could also use char-grilled, skinned peppers and a little fruity vinegar. Sweet red peppers, hot red chillies and red paprika powder are all integral to the cuisines of many of Germany's neighbouring countries.

500 g prepared sauerkraut

100 g long grain white rice

1 white cabbage, about 750 g–1 kg

3 onions, chopped

2 teaspoons caraway seeds

1 large bunch of fresh thyme

1½–2 teaspoons salt

500 g minced pork, bacon or ham

50 g salted butter, cubed

4 ripe tomatoes, chopped

100 g tomato passata

2 tablespoons tomato concentrate

about 400 g canned roasted, skinned pimientos, chopped

½ teaspoon cayenne pepper

6–8 rindless rashers smoked streaky bacon (optional)

Serves 4–5

1 Drain the sauerkraut, and rinse in cold water if very sharp tasting. Squeeze dry and spread half over the base of a large baking dish. Cook the rice in boiling salted water for 10 minutes or until part-cooked. Drain and set aside.

2 Cut the central core out of the cabbage and peel off 16 perfect leaves. Blanch in a large pan of boiling water until limp, 2 at a time (2–3 minutes for outer leaves, less for inner ones). Refresh in cold water, then drain.

3 Mix 2 of the chopped onions with the caraway, thyme, salt, a quarter of the pork and half the remaining sauerkraut. Mix in a food processor, then knead, with the cooked rice, into the remaining pork. Divide into 16.

4 Snip and discard the hard central rib from each leaf. Shape the 16 portions of mixture and put one at the base of each leaf. Roll up, turn and tuck in the side flaps, and continue to roll up like a cork, with the seams underneath.

5 To make the sauce, heat the butter in a pan and cook the remaining onion until golden. Add the tomatoes, passata, tomato concentrate, pimiento and cayenne. Cook for 3–4 minutes. Put in a blender and purée until smooth.

6 Put some of the sauce into a baking tin, add the rolls, sauerkraut and bacon, if using, cover with foil and cook in a preheated oven at 180°C (350°F) Gas Mark 4 for 1 hour. Uncover and cook for 30 minutes. Serve, drizzled with sauce.

honey rice ice cream
with orange and saffron

125 g white short grain pudding rice

600 ml fresh orange juice

175 g clear honey

1 large pinch of powdered saffron

600 ml whipping cream

1 tablespoon Cointreau, Grand Marnier
or triple sec liqueur

2 teaspoons fresh orange zest,
cut in fine shreds with a
cannelle knife or zester

Serves 4–6

An unusual ice cream which, instead of being made of egg-based custard, fruit and cream, is made of short or round grain rice cooked in orange juice until it is so tender it forms a jelly-like custard. One caution, however, is that starch-based ices need slow 'conditioning' in the fridge for an hour rather than being eaten straight from the freezer (too brittle) or thawed quickly at room temperature (too soft outside, too firm inside). So 'condition' the ice cream in the refrigerator while earlier courses are served. A delicious, easy, exotic recipe.

Combine the rice, 450 ml of the orange juice and 50 ml boiling water in a medium saucepan. Bring to the boil, reduce the heat, cover and simmer on the lowest possible heat for about 20 minutes until the rice is tender and the liquid greatly reduced. Stir well, and allow to cool over ice for 5–10 minutes. Stir in the honey, remaining juice, saffron powder, cream, liqueur and zest, and stir again.

Prepare the ice cream making machine and, with the paddles turning, pour in the mixture. Churn for 18–20 minutes or until the mixture becomes solid enough to make a rhythmic rattling noise as the blade rotates.

Smooth the ice cream into a 1 litre domed metal bombe mould, Pyrex bowl or loaf tin. Cover and refreeze the ice cream for 2 hours or longer.

One hour before serving, put in the refrigerator to soften. Remove the lid. Hold warmed, wet cloths around the mould or dip it briefly into hand-hot water. Invert then turn out the ice cream. Serve in slices with crisp biscuits or wafers.

To still-freeze in a home freezer: set freezer to 'fast-freeze' on its lowest setting. Pour the mixture into a non-rigid polypropylene 1 litre container. Snap on the lid. Fast-freeze for 1½ hours or until the mixture forms hard crystals around the edge but is soft at the centre. Whisk the edges into the centre using an electric or balloon whisk. Reseal.

Alternatively, empty the part-set ice cream into a food processor. Process to a uniform slush. Pour back into the container. Reseal. Refreeze for 1½ hours. Repeat the beating. Refreeze for a final 2 hours or so.

The cooking traditions of the Middle East are inextricably bound to their historical links with the great civilizations of **Persia** and **Byzantium**. Dishes such as pilafs and pulaus migrated across the world to become paella in Spain and even jambalaya in the USA.

the middle east

A classic dish, usually made in 3 or 4 separate operations, is slightly simplified here into a one-pan dish. A great party dish that looks impressive, but is easy once the initial stages are complete.

zarda palau

chicken pulau with almonds, orange and pistachios

2 oranges, washed and dried*
175 g granulated sugar
2 large pinches saffron threads
or 4 pinches saffron powder
50 g butter ghee or butter
125 g blanched almonds
4–6 boneless, skinless breasts
of chicken or guinea fowl,
each cut into 4 pieces
2 onions, sliced into rings
500 g white basmati rice
50 g pistachio nuts,
blanched and skinned
salt and freshly ground black pepper
6–8 sprigs of mint, to garnish
Serves 4–6

*If minneolas are in season and available, substitute 4 of these for the 2 oranges. Their juice is good, but their zest is superb!

Using a zester or canelle knife, remove the orange zest in long shreds or, alternatively, use a vegetable peeler, then slice the strips into fine shreds. Blanch by pouring over boiling water, then refresh in cold water and drain.

Put the sugar in a pan with the orange zest and about 175 ml juice and boil for 5–8 minutes, until thick and syrupy. Add the saffron, stir and set aside.

Heat the butter or butter ghee in a large flameproof casserole. Briefly brown the almonds, remove with a slotted spoon and set aside. Add the chicken or guinea fowl, brown for about 2–3 minutes on each side, then remove and set aside.

Add the onions and cook over moderate heat until softened and translucent. Return the chicken to the pan, add seasonings and 1 litre boiling water, then stir to dissolve the sediment. Stir in the rice and return to the boil. Cover with a lid, reduce to a simmer, then cook gently for 12–15 minutes on top of the stove or 35–45 minutes in a preheated oven at 150°C (300°F) Gas Mark 2. Remove the lid: the rice should be fairly plump and tender and the liquid absorbed.

Sprinkle with the almonds, pistachios and saffron syrup mixture, reserving the zest. Cover and cook again for a further 5 minutes on the hob or 10–15 minutes in the oven. Add the reserved zest, looping it up attractively on top. Add the mint garnish and serve hot from the casserole.

Crisp salad leaves, bunches of herbs, hot flatbread and a large bowl of plain yoghurt will all make wonderful accompaniments.

The author and Middle Eastern food expert, Tess Mallos, described this ancient rice dish as one which perfectly satisfied the calorie and blood-sugar needs of Bahrain's pearl divers who dived, in hazardous conditions, to considerable depths and sustained each quest for 10 minutes at a time. The combination of richness, sweetness and savouriness is remarkable and intriguing. Traditionally this dish would be served with lamb or seafood dishes.

pearl divers' rice
with saffron and honey

1 pinch of saffron threads
or 1 large pinch of powdered saffron
8 green cardamom pods, crushed
2 tablespoons rosewater
1 litre boiling lamb or chicken stock
500 g white basmati rice
2 onions, sliced into rings
2 teaspoons salt
75 g clear honey
50 g butter ghee or butter,
chopped into 8 pieces
1 large bunch of fresh parsley, dill or
mint, scissor-snipped (optional)
Serves 4–6

Combine the saffron, the black seeds from the cardamom pods, rosewater and 4 tablespoons of the boiling stock in a small heatproof bowl, and set over boiling water while you cook the rice.

Put the rice, onions and salt in a large, heavy-based pan, and pour over the remaining boiling stock. Return to the boil, cover, reduce to a gentle simmer and cook for 10 minutes or until almost all the liquid has been absorbed.

Pour the saffron-cardamom-rosewater-stock mixture on top and drizzle the honey over the surface. Push 8 holes in the rice down to the base of the pan and add a bit of ghee or butter to each. Cover the pan again and simmer for a further 5 minutes. Remove from the heat, wrap the pan in a cloth, leave to stand for another 10 minutes, then serve hot, sprinkled with parsley, dill or mint, if using.

This is an easy, modern update of a traditional long-cooked Iranian dish. The spice seasoning, *baharat*, is an important component: use the extra with other dishes. Keep it airtight in a screwtop jar or lidded china pot and bring it to the table as a condiment for sprinkling.

lamb and rice sausage
with parsley, lime and spices

1 large bunch of flat leaf parsley

1 large bunch of fresh coriander

500 g twice-minced lamb

4 garlic cloves, crushed

1 onion, finely sliced

2 teaspoons sea salt

2 tablespoons ground cinnamon

250 g cooked brown rice

Lime and Lamb Stock:

600 ml boiling lamb stock

1 large bunch of parsley stalks, crushed

zest (in big pieces) and juice

of 1 lime

Baharat Seasoning:

1 tablespoon black peppercorns

1 tablespoon coriander seeds

1 tablespoon cumin seeds

1 tablespoon cloves

1 cinnamon stick

2 tablespoons hot paprika

½ nutmeg, grated

Serves 4

Scissor-snip the parsley and coriander. Mix with the lamb, garlic, onion, salt, cinnamon and cooked rice. Knead to make a dense, smooth paste then divide into 6 pieces. Using clean hands, roll out each piece to about 20 cm long. Coil this up on a flat, heatproof plate, such as Pyrex. Continue shaping the lengths of sausage, joining each new section firmly to the last using a fork. The completed coil should be about 30 cm diameter. Put a deep, heavy-based frying pan or shallow flameproof casserole upside down over the plate, then invert both – the sausage will be compressed by the plate as it cooks.

Pour the boiling stock over the sausage in the frying pan, crush the parsley stalks and add to the pan together with the lime zest. Bring the pan back to the boil (8–10 minutes), reduce to a steady simmer, cover and cook for 20 minutes more.

To make the *baharat* seasoning, put all the ingredients in an electric spice grinder or food processor and whizz. Reserve 2 tablespoons for this dish and store the rest for later use in other dishes.

When the sausage is cooked, strain off the liquid. Put a plate over the pan, invert both, then remove the pan. Slide the sausage off the plate and on to a serving dish. Pour over the lime juice and sprinkle with the *baharat*. Serve with crisp green leafy salad and buttered or saffron-scented rice.

Note: Brown rice cooks particularly quickly in a pressure cooker. Allow about 15–20 minutes, (about a third of the usual cooking time), following the manufacturer's instructions.

stuffed vegetables
with rice and sour cherries

Persian seasonings are fascinating and refreshing. This dish has a spicing mixture which hinges on pepper, cinnamon and mint (known as *nano dok*), together with turmeric, cumin and sumak, a red-brown souring powder. Dried barberries or dried sour cherries can be difficult to find, so dried cranberries could be used instead.

However, all these ingredients are available in Middle Eastern foodstores, Iranian grocers, specialist delis and the more enlightened supermarkets! Both short and long grain white rice (basmati is a favourite) work well in this homely but delicious vegetable dish.

4 large beefsteak tomatoes, with the tops sliced off and reserved
4 large peppers, with stems
2 tablespoons butter ghee or clarified butter
2 garlic cloves, chopped
2 onions, chopped
250 g twice-minced lamb
2 cinnamon sticks, crushed
I teaspoon ground turmeric
I teaspoon cumin seeds, crushed
I teaspoon cracked black pepper
I teaspoon sumak (optional)
50 g dried sour cherries, barberries or cranberries
100 g white short grain, basmati or other long grain rice
100 g bulgar (burghul, or cracked wheat
750 ml lamb or chicken stock
½ teaspoon salt
2 teaspoons dried mint or 2 tablespoon sliced fresh mint
To Serve (optional):
8 sprigs of mint
250 g sheep or goat's milk yoghurt
lavash, taftoon, pitta or other Middle Eastern flatbreads
Serves 4

1 Scoop the tomato pulp and seeds into a blender. Halve the peppers and remove and discard the seeds and membranes. Roast the vegetable halves in a preheated oven at 200°C (400°F) Gas Mark 6 for 10 minutes.

2 Meanwhile heat the ghee or butter in a heavy-based pan and sauté the garlic, onions, minced lamb, cinnamon sticks, turmeric, cumin, pepper and sumak, if using, for 5–6 minutes over high heat, stirring regularly.

3 Whizz the tomato pulp and seeds in the blender, and add to the pan together with the dried fruit, rice, bulgar wheat and 600 ml of the stock. Season with salt. Return to the boil, cover, then simmer for 10 minutes.

4 Spoon the mixture into the vegetable shells and spoon 1 tablespoon of reserved stock over each. Set the sliced tops back on top of the tomatoes. Cover the dish with double layer of foil and return to the oven.

5 Reduce the oven heat to 180°C (350°F) Gas Mark 5 and cook for about 40–45 minutes or until the rice is plumped up, all liquid is absorbed and the vegetables smell sweetly aromatic.

6 Serve hot with a spoonful of yoghurt on top if liked (remove the tops of the tomatoes first then replace at an angle). Sprinkle with fresh or dried mint and serve with sprigs of mint and flatbreads to mop up the juices.

Traditionally this dish used almond 'milk' obtained from grinding blanched almonds, infusing them in liquid, then squeezing out their liquid to use in the dish. The almonds were then discarded. Almonds are expensive, so I infuse them, but do not discard them. This gives a slightly grittier, grainier version, but delicious nonetheless. Some people loathe the marzipan taste of almond essence, so you could use Noyau or Amaretto liqueur instead.

keskül
almond rice custard
with berries or pomegranate seeds

750 ml milk
100 g very fresh ground almonds
I large pinch of salt
50 g ground rice
150 ml single cream
75 g caster sugar
⅛–¼ teaspoon almond essence or
2–3 teaspoons Noyau liqueur
To Serve:
I ripe pomegranate, or
175 g soft berries, such as
blackberries, mulberries,
red or white currants
25 g pistachio nuts or toasted almond
flakes (optional)
15 g icing sugar (optional)
Serves 4–6

Boil 250 ml of the milk until frothing, pour on to the ground almonds, stir well, then pour the mixture into a blender or food processor. Whizz for 10 seconds.

Mix the salt, ground rice and cream. Heat the remaining milk until frothing. Pour on to the ground rice and cream mixture, then whisk. Return to the pan, bring to the boil, then simmer, stirring, for 2–3 minutes or until thickened. Add the unstrained almond-milk mixture, and the sugar.

Continue cooking and stirring briefly, then remove from the heat. Cool the custard over iced water. When almost cold stir in the almond essence or liqueur to suit your taste. Pour into 4–6 small dishes, bowls or glasses. Chill.

If using a pomegranate, break it open, remove the clumps of red seeds and scatter a pile in the centre of each bowl. If using berries, remove the stems and place in the same way.

Sprinkle with almonds and dust with icing sugar, if using. Serve warm, cool or chilled: it thickens more on standing. Crisp biscuits would also be a suitable accompaniment.

From Morocco to the Cape, from **West Africa to Zanzibar**, African cuisines are enormously diverse. They range from the **Islamic-influenced** dishes of North Africa, to the Indian-spiced curries of the east coasts, and the **traditions** taken west to the Americas on slave ships.

africa

Spice-trading nations like Portugal, India and Iraq have had strong influences on the varied and lively cuisine of the eastern coast of Africa. This simple curry uses good quality curry paste and a purée of sun-dried tomatoes, which produces interesting effects. Use white fish such as gurnard, snapper or bream. Use a non-stick pan so the rice will reheat perfectly without sticking.

tanzanian fish curry
with mustard seed rice

4 pieces white fish, about 175 g each

1 tablespoon turmeric

1 teaspoon sea salt flakes

3 tablespoons groundnut oil

2 onions, sliced into rings

2 garlic cloves, crushed

2 tablespoons medium-hot curry paste

3 tablespoons sun-dried tomato paste

2 green jalapeño or serrano chillies

2 limes

400 ml canned coconut milk

Mustard Seed Rice:

2 tablespoons groundnut oil

4 garlic cloves, crushed

1–2 tablespoons black mustard seeds

1 cinnamon stick, crushed (optional)

750 g cooked white long grain rice

3–4 tablespoons seasoned fish stock

Serves 4

Pat the fish dry with kitchen paper, then rub it with the turmeric and salt. Heat the oil in a large pan and brown the fish briefly on both sides. Remove the fish from the pan. Add the onions and garlic, sauté until browned, then sauté the curry paste and tomato paste for 1–2 minutes. Halve the chillies lengthways and deseed, then add them to the pan together with the juice of 1 of the limes. Cook another 2 minutes, taking care not to burn. Add the coconut milk and heat to simmering. Add the fish and poach for 5–6 minutes on each side, adding a little water if the sauce becomes too thick.

To prepare the rice, heat the oil in a non-stick pan and sauté the garlic, seeds and cinnamon, if using, until the seeds start to pop and the garlic and cinnamon smell aromatic. Add the rice and stir-fry, moving it constantly, for 3–4 minutes. Add the well seasoned stock, cover the pan and heat the rice through.

Serve the seeded rice in deep bowls, with the curry spooned over. Garnish with the remaining lime, cut into wedges or chunks.

Flavourful chicken, stewed in a tomato, peanut and chilli sauce, is a West African favourite. This Mali version has brilliant orange-red dendé oil (palm oil) stirred into both the stew and the rice. Vivid colour and a strange, pungent earthy flavour is the result. If no palm oil is available (try ethnic markets and Afro-Caribbean grocers) substitute a little extra groundnut oil mixed with annatto powder or even turmeric.

chicken and peanut stew
with red dendé rice

1.25 kg chicken
1 teaspoon cayenne pepper
1–2 teaspoons salt
1 tablespoon ground ginger
1 tablespoon mild paprika
2 tablespoons groundnut oil
2 onions, each cut into 8 wedges
4 garlic cloves, chopped
400 g canned tomatoes in juice
4 ripe tomatoes, cut into chunks
1 large bunch of fresh oregano,
or 1½ teaspoons dried
4 tablespoons crunchy peanut butter
1 litre hot chicken stock
400 g white long grain rice
2–3 tablespoons red dendé (palm) oil
1 lemon or lime, cut in 4 wedges

Serves 4–6

Cut the chicken into 10–12 pieces. Combine the cayenne, salt, ginger and paprika in a bowl, add the chicken and turn until well coated. Heat the groundnut oil in a large deep flameproof pan, add half the chicken and sauté for about 3–4 minutes or until browned. Remove the browned chicken pieces from the pan and keep them warm. Repeat with the remaining chicken, remove and keep it warm.

Sauté the onion and garlic briefly, then return all the chicken to the pan. Chop the canned tomatoes, and add them to the pan together with the fresh tomatoes, oregano (keeping a few sprigs for garnish, if fresh), peanut butter and 300 ml of the hot chicken stock. Return to the boil, reduce to a simmer, part-cover the pan and cook for 30 minutes.

Meanwhile put the rice in a medium, heavy-based saucepan together with the remaining hot chicken stock. Return to the boil, cover, reduce the heat to very low and cook for another 12 minutes or until all liquid is absorbed. Stir in about 1–2 tablespoons of the dendé oil and set aside.

Add the remaining dendé oil to the stew, and stir well. Serve the stew and rice together with a wedge of lemon or lime and a sprig of oregano, if using.

COUSCOUS

moroccan couscous

with rice, lemon and tahini

A simplified version of the classic Moroccan dish *Couscous aux Sept Légumes* – use courgettes, pattypan squash, or both. Pickled lemons, instant couscous and harissa, the fiery red North African spice paste can be found in North African, Middle Eastern and French grocers, ethnic foodstores and good supermarkets.

Halve the courgettes lengthways and the squash crossways. Peel and deseed the cucumber and cut into chunks. Slice the carrots diagonally. Mix the chermoula ingredients in a bowl, add the vegetables and toss until well coated. Leave to stand.

Put the rice and hot stock into a medium, heavy-based pan, return to the boil, cover, reduce to a simmer and cook, undisturbed, for 6 minutes. Stir in the couscous and arrange the vegetables evenly on top. Sprinkle over the remaining chermoula and other juices.

Cover and cook, undisturbed, for a further 8–10 minutes or until the vegetables are succulent and tender, the couscous and rice are cooked, and all the liquid is absorbed.

Reserve 3–4 sprigs of the mint and chop the rest. Put the vegetables on one side of the serving dish. Stir the olives, lemon pieces (or zest) and chopped mint through the rice-couscous mix. Spoon on to the serving dish beside the vegetables, and leave to cool slightly. To make the tahini sauce, put the garlic, cumin, tahini and lemon juice in a blender and purée to a thick cream. Trickle in 8–10 tablespoons iced water, a spoonful at a time to form a pale creamy dressing.

To serve, trickle the sauce over the salad (warm or cool, but not chilled), add the reserved mint sprigs, and serve the remaining dressing separately. Delicious!

8–12 baby courgettes or pattypan squash

½ cucumber

4 carrots

250 g white long grain rice

900 ml hot, seasoned vegetable stock

125 g 'instant' couscous

Chermoula Marinade:

2 garlic cloves, chopped

2 teaspoons harissa paste

1 teaspoon powdered cumin

1 teaspoon mild paprika

1 bunch fresh coriander, snipped

6 tablespoons fruity olive oil

Tahini Sauce:

2 garlic cloves, crushed

1 teaspoon cumin

125 g tahini (roasted sesame) paste

juice of 2 lemons

To Serve:

100 g small black olives

½ preserved lemon, diced, or lemon zest

1 large bunch of fresh mint

Serves 4

It was in India, many centuries ago, that rice was first parboiled to increase its hardness and keeping qualities, as well as its nutritional value – a crucial consideration in a country where **vegetarianism** is very much part of the **cultural** and **religious** tradition.

india,
pakistan
and sri lanka

orange and pumpkin pulao
with two cashumbers and a raita

Rice is the staple food of much of India. The best-known varieties are the short, fine-grained *jeera*, the parboiled *golden sela* basmati, good for pulaos, the fruity scented *ambre mohue* from Maharashtra, and *punni*, a long grain rice from Tamil Nadu. Basmati rice, originally from Afghanistan, now grows in the Punjab, Haryana, the foothills of the Himalayas and Uttar Pradesh, as well as in Pakistan, the US and Thailand, though there are slight regional differences. It is used for ceremonial dishes because it is more expensive. Year-old basmati rice is much prized – some gourmands age their rice as connoisseurs age wines.

50 g butter ghee

I onion, sliced

200 g basmati rice

I fresh bay leaf, crushed

I cinnamon stick

4 cloves

12 cardamom pods, crushed

250 g peeled, deseeded pumpkin

finely sliced zest and juice of 2 oranges

Carrot and Coconut Cashumber:

75 g fresh coconut or 3 tablespoons

desiccated coconut (see method)

250 g carrots, coarsely grated

100 g roasted peanuts, chopped

juice of 2 limes

½ teaspoon salt

2 chillies, deseeded and chopped

2 tablespoons groundnut oil

I teaspoon cumin seeds

I teaspoon black mustard seeds

Onion and Tomato Cashumber:

2 red onions, finely sliced

2 tomatoes, sliced

I teaspoon toasted sesame seeds

I tablespoon soft brown sugar

Cucumber Raita:

½ cucumber, diced

2 cloves garlic, crushed

I tablespoon chopped fresh mint

125 ml thick plain yoghurt

I tablespoon groundnut oil

I tablespoon mustard seeds

Serves 4

Heat the butter ghee in a pan, add the onion and fry to a deep golden brown. Add the rice, bay leaf, cinnamon, cloves and black seeds from the cardamom pods. Sauté for another 2 minutes. Cut the pumpkin into I cm dice, and add to the pan with 450 ml of boiling salted water.

Return to the boil, cover and reduce the heat to as low as possible. Cook, undisturbed, for about 10 minutes. Add the orange zest and juice, cover, cook for 2–3 minutes more, turn off the heat and leave to stand.

To make the carrot and coconut cashumber, grate the fresh coconut. If no fresh coconut is available, use desiccated coconut, briefly blanched in boiling water, then drained. Mix in a small bowl with the carrots, chopped peanuts, lime juice, salt and chillies, and stir well.

In a separate pan heat 2 tablespoons of groundnut oil (or mustard oil if you can find it). Add the cumin seeds and black mustard seeds, heat until they start to pop, then pour over the cashumber.

To make the onion and tomato cashumber, put the sliced onion in a heatproof bowl, and pour over boiling water. Refresh under cold water and pat dry on kitchen paper. Mix in a small serving bowl together with the sliced tomato, sesame seeds and brown sugar.

To make the raita, mix the cucumber in a bowl with the garlic, mint and yoghurt. Heat the groundnut (or mustard) oil in a small pan, add the mustard seeds and fry briefly until they pop. Spoon over the raita.

Serve the two cashumbers and the raita as accompaniments to the pulao.

Many of the pilafs and biryanis from the state of Gujerat, in north-west India, contain ambitious spice combinations, a legacy of its past position on a major caravan route with famed culinary wealth and riches. Gujerat is largely vegetarian, and rice dishes are often made with Moghul-Arab influences of nuts and dried fruits. Asafoetida, a common Indian spice, stinks on its own, but has the uncanny ability to enhance other flavours.

spicy seeded pilaf
with okra and spinach

1 onion
250 g pattypan squash
1–1½ teaspoons hot chilli powder
½ teaspoon ground turmeric
2 tablespoons groundnut oil or ghee
1 teaspoon poppy seeds, crushed
1 teaspoon cumin seeds, crushed
1 teaspoon coriander seeds, crushed
½ teaspoon asafoetida (optional)
4 garlic cloves, crushed
¼ teaspoon salt
250 g white basmati rice
600 ml boiling vegetable stock
2 dried bay leaves (optional)
25 g creamed coconut, chopped
125 g okra, trimmed
125 g baby spinach
125 g fresh green peas (optional)
50 g coconut shreds (fresh or dried)
Serves 4

Slice the onion lengthways into thin segments. Toss the onion and pattypans in the chilli and turmeric. Heat the oil and sauté the vegetables for 1–2 minutes or until aromatic. Add the poppy, cumin and coriander seeds, the asafoetida, garlic and salt. Cook over moderate heat until the seeds begin to crackle and pop and become aromatic.

Stir in the rice. Sauté for another minute, stirring gently, then add the stock, bay leaves, if using, and the creamed coconut. Cover and reduce the heat to simmering, then cook undisturbed for 8 minutes.

Add the okra, spinach, green peas and coconut shreds. Cover and cook for a further 4–5 minutes until the rice is tender but dry. Remove the bay leaves, stir well and serve the rice with meat, poultry or fish curries and accompaniments such as the cashumbers and raita on page 83.

Mild and creamy Indian kormas are a legacy of Moghul rule in India. Their elegance and opulence demonstrate their grand, imperial past – and make them perfect special-occasion dishes.

chicken korma
with pistachio basmati rice

250 g sweet potato, sliced

250 g baby sweet corn cobs

125 g sugar snap peas

125 g French beans

1 teaspoon white peppercorns

2 teaspoons sea salt flakes

20 green cardamom pods

2 tablespoons white poppy seeds

4 garlic cloves, finely sliced

20 g fresh ginger, finely sliced

½ teaspoon ground turmeric

¼–½ teaspoon cayenne pepper

125 g cashew nuts

75 g pine nuts

400 ml coconut milk

100 g thick, plain Greek yoghurt

2 tablespoons lime pickle

1 spicy stock cube, crumbled

375 g cooked, boneless chicken, cut into 1 cm cubes

Pistachio Basmati Rice:

500 g basmati rice

25 g pistachio nuts

6 tablespoons torn coriander leaves

Serves 4–6

Put the sweet potato and sweet corn in a pan of boiling water and parboil for 3 minutes. Drain. Blanch the sugar snap peas and French beans for 1 minute, cool under running water, then drain. Using a mortar and pestle, pound the peppercorns, salt and cardamom pods. Discard the empty green pods, and reserve the black seeds. Put the mortar contents in a food processor with the white poppy seeds, garlic, ginger, turmeric, cayenne pepper, half the cashew nuts and half the pine nuts. Whizz to a rough paste. Add the coconut milk, thick Greek yoghurt and lime pickle. Whizz again until fairly smooth.

Pour into a large pan, bring to the boil, reduce the heat, and simmer for 5 minutes, adding the crumbled stock cube, 300 ml of boiling water and remaining cashews (but not the pine nuts).

Add the parboiled corn cobs and sweet potato, the blanched peas and beans, and the chicken cubes to the sauce. Simmer for 3–4 minutes, until fragrant and hot.

Bring the rice to the boil in double its volume of boiling salted water. Simmer, covered, for 12 minutes or until all the water is absorbed. Blanch, skin and sliver the pistachios, then add to the rice together with the coriander and remaining pine nuts. Leave the rice to stand for 1–2 minutes. Serve with the korma.

gosht biryani

lamb biryani
with coriander and cinnamon

Another elegant culinary result of Moghul rule in India. Because the lamb must first be cooked until tender (and the stock used to cook the rice), this stage can be done well in advance, even the day before. Indian cooks always cut their onions into wedges lengthways, a method that produces pretty shapes and good caramelized edges, and is also worth using in Western-style dishes. Serve this dish with accompaniments such a spicy sambal or mango chutney.

2 whole green chillies, pierced

I kg boneless leg of lamb

750 ml water or stock

I bunch of coriander stems

5 cm piece root ginger, sliced

2 cinnamon sticks, crushed

I teaspoon salt, or to taste

125 g clarified butter or ghee

4 onions, sliced into wedges

black seeds from 2 teaspoons green cardamom pods, crushed

I teaspoon cloves

½ teaspoon ground turmeric

2 teaspoons cumin seeds, crushed

2 teaspoons coriander seeds

2 red or yellow peppers, quartered, deseeded and cored

75 g cauliflower florets

175 g courgettes

300 g white basmati rice

4 garlic cloves, finely sliced

I large pinch of saffron threads

75 g. shelled pistachio nuts

I large bunch of coriander

Serves 4

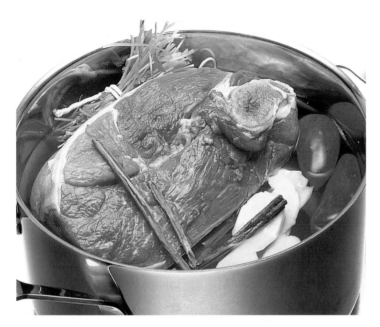

1 Place the first 5 ingredients and 1 cinnamon stick in a large saucepan. Bring to the boil, cover and reduce a simmer. Cook for 1¼–1½ hours until the lamb is very tender. Remove and cube the lamb. Measure 600 ml of stock.

2 Heat the butter or ghee in a pan and fry the onion 2–3 minutes until golden. Add the remaining spices and fry over a moderate heat until the seeds begin to pop. Remove the onions with a slotted spoon and set aside.

3 Add the pepper, cauliflower and courgette pieces to the pan and fry for 1–2 minutes. Remove with a slotted spoon. Add the rice and garlic. Stir over moderate heat for 2 minutes, until well coated with butter and spices.

4 Transfer the rice mixture to a large saucepan, then add layers of the onion, lamb and spiced vegetables. Pour in the lamb stock, return the boil, then reduce to a gentle simmer.

5 Sprinkle in the saffron threads, cover with a lid, and cook for 15 minutes or until all the liquid is absorbed. Blanch the pistachios, then add to the pan with the sprigs of coriander. Cover with a lid and turn off the heat.

6 Cover the pan with a cloth, then let stand, covered, for 10 minutes on top of the stove. Alternatively, put the pan in a preheated oven at 180°C (350°F) Gas Mark 4 for 10 minutes. Serve with chutneys and a raita.

A recipe with ingredients typical of the former Portuguese colony of Goa; olive oil, cashews and pork. Pork is forbidden to Muslims and cattle sacred to Hindus, but both are acceptable to the many Goans who are Christians, and their fine cuisine includes both pork and beef. Most Indian cooks would make their own garam masala, but it is also widely available in Asian stores.

gingered pork chop masala
with cashew rice

---

5 cm root ginger
I small medium-hot red chilli
I onion, chopped
4 garlic cloves, crushed
I teaspoon garam masala
6 tablespoons fresh lemon juice
I teaspoon turmeric powder
I teaspoon salt
2 tablespoons brown sugar
I large bunch of fresh mint
4–6 boneless pork chops, about 750 g
2 tablespoons virgin olive oil
150 ml fresh orange juice
4 tablespoons thick coconut milk
8 tablespoons thick yoghurt

Cashew Rice:

200 g patna or basmati rice
450 ml boiling meat or chicken stock
125 g roasted, salted cashew nuts

Serves 4

Peel the ginger and slice finely. Deseed the chilli and chop finely. Put the ginger, chilli, onion, garlic, garam masala, lemon juice, turmeric, salt, sugar and half the mint in a blender or food processor and blend to a thick purée. Reserve half and pour the remainder over the pork. Leave to marinate while you cook the rice.

Put the rice in a pan with the boiling stock, bring to the boil, reduce to a simmer, cover the pan and cook, undisturbed, for 12–15 minutes or until tender. (The liquid should be completely absorbed, and the rice tender.)

Heat the oil in a frying pan and cook the marinated pork for 3–4 minutes on each side. Add the orange juice, cover and cook gently for 3–4 minutes longer. Stir in the coconut milk and 2 tablespoons yoghurt and simmer until creamy.

Put the cashew nuts and 2 tablespoons of the remaining yoghurt in the food processor with most of the remaining mint (leave the best sprigs for garnish). Blend to a creamy purée, then stir into the rice, together with the reserved marinade. Serve the pork and its sauce over the cashew-rice, scatter with the reserved sprigs of mint and trail the remaining yoghurt over the top.

Serve with chapattis, green beans or okra, a dhaal of split peas, perhaps, and a cool, crisp green salad.

Note: Palm sugar or jaggery may be substituted for the brown sugar, and lime juice for the lemon juice, if preferred.

Best-known of India's superb condensed milk puddings is *kheer*, though regional versions have other names. Holy texts tell of these dishes being offered to the gods. Cardamom, pistachio nuts, rose or almond essence and Indian kewra water (made from pandanus leaves) may also be added, as well as sugar in various forms. A sumptuous pudding, wonderful served warm, cool or chilled. Varak – real silver, hand-beaten into paper-fine sheets – is available from Asian delis or specialist grocers. It adds drama to this already exotic dish.

kheer rice pudding
with cardamom and pine nuts

40 g butter ghee or unsalted butter
40 g white basmati rice,
washed, drained and air-dried
2 fresh bay leaves, crushed
2 litres full-cream milk
100 g light muscovado sugar
75 g currants or raisins
12 green cardamom pods, crushed,
black seeds removed, pods discarded
25 g toasted pine nuts
1–2 sheets thin silver foil (varak)
(optional, for special occasions)

Serves 4

Heat the butter ghee or butter over moderate heat in a large, wide, heavy-based, preferably non-stick 5 litre saucepan. Stir-fry the rice until it darkens to pale gold, then add the bay leaves and milk. Increase the heat to high and, stirring constantly, bring to a frothing boi (about 10–12 minutes). Reduce the heat slightly to medium high.

Let the milk boil for another 35–40 minutes, until reduced to about half the original volume. Add sugar, currants and cardamom, and continue to cook on a low heat, stirring often, for another 15–20 minutes, until reduced to about $1/3$–$1/4$ of its original volume. Stir and cool over iced water, then chill.

Decorate with nuts and silver foil, if using, lifting the foil on its attached tissue paper, inverting it over the pudding, then pulling off the amount needed using a fine brush. The pieces do not need to be immaculate – fragments look good.

Rice flour is used here with an equal quantity of plain flour, giving a delicate crispness to these little biscuits. They are delicious with coffee or mint tea, or served with ice creams, custards or sorbets. Edible ricepaper (another rice product) is often used in cooking biscuits or sweets.

elaiche gaja

spiced shortbread biscuits
with rosewater and pistachios

250 g salted butter, at room temperature

1 teaspoon black cardamom seeds (from 8–10 green cardamom pods, lightly crushed)

125 g caster sugar

150 g rice flour

150 g plain flour

25 g blanched, skinned pistachios, finely slivered or chopped

¼ teaspoon salt

¼ teaspoon baking powder

1 teaspoon double strength rosewater or almond essence

2–3 sheets ricepaper (optional)

2 teaspoons blanched pistachios, slivered, to decorate

Makes 32

Cut the butter into small pieces, and put in a food processor with the black cardamom seeds. Work them together in small bursts, gradually adding the sugar through the feed tube until the mixture becomes light and fluffy.

Mix the rice and plain flours with the ground pistachios, salt and baking powder. Add a quarter of this mixture at a time down the feed tube, using the pulse button, until a soft crumbly dough results. Alternatively, use a bowl and a whisk. Turn out the dough on to a floured work surface and mix in the rosewater by hand. Put the dough on a sheet of teflon fabric, bakewell paper or ricepaper, and pat out into a rectangle about 25 x 20 cm. Using a knife, mark into 32 evenly sized rectangles, about 6 x 2.5 cm each. Prick all over with a fork. Sprinkle a few slivers of pistachio over each biscuit, then bake in a preheated oven at 120°C (250°F) Gas Mark ½ for 1 hour or until pale gold, crisp but not deep brown. Remove from the oven and separate each biscuit, cutting cleanly through the ricepaper as well, if used. Cool on a wire rack and, when completely cold, store in an airtight container.

spicy coconut loaf
with cashew nuts and cardamom

A densely textured cake, based on a Sri Lankan recipe. You can vary the spices, chopped almonds or walnuts could replace the cashews, and lemon zest and juice can be used instead of orange. This cake can also double as a quick pudding, served with snowy coconut sorbet.

Grease and paper-line a 500 g loaf tin (about 20 x 12 x 8 cm). Put the coconut and water in a blender (in 2 batches, if necessary) and whizz until creamy. Set aside. Using an electric mixer, whisk the egg yolks, 1 tablespoon of the coconut mixture and the sugar until light and fluffy. Add the remaining coconut mixture and beat well by hand. Sift in the flour, ground rice and baking powder, then add the black cardamom seeds, spices, orange flower water, cashew nuts and orange zest – but not the juice – and stir well. Whisk the egg whites in a clean bowl until they form stiff peaks. Add the second measure of sugar and whisk again until the meringue is stiff and shiny. Fold it gently into the coconut mixture. Pour into the prepared loaf tin. Put towards the top of a preheated oven and bake at 160°C (325°F) Gas Mark 3 for 1 hour 10 minutes, or until risen and golden brown on top. A skewer inserted in the centre of the loaf should come out clean. Pour the juice over the top. Leave to stand 15 minutes, then turn out of the tin on to a wire rack. Cool a little and serve warm, or cool completely and store in an airtight container.

butter, for greasing
140 g desiccated coconut
350 ml water
2 eggs, separated
250 g caster sugar
75 g self-raising flour
200 g ground rice
1 teaspoon baking powder
12 green cardamom pods, crushed, black
seeds reserved, pods discarded
½ teaspoon ground cloves
½ teaspoon ground cinnamon
½ teaspoon ground nutmeg
1 teaspoon double-strength
orange flower water
75 g cashew nuts, chopped
finely sliced zest and juice of 1 orange
(keep separate)
25 g caster sugar
Makes 500 g loaf

the far east
and south-east asia

Rice is a staple food in China, Japan and South-east Asia, and has achieved an almost **mythic status**. Few meals would be complete without rice in one of its many forms – as the original grain, or as noodles, wrappers, vinegar or even wine. Rice cooking in these regions has achieved the status of **high art**.

classic cantonese fried rice
with spring onions, ham and crab

This casual homely dish is easy to make as long as the rice has been recently cooked and cool (neither chilled nor still hot) and you keep the eggs creamy. My version uses ham and crab, chilli and black bean sauces, as well as tomato juice to give a rosy effect. Stirring sauces through the rice, rather than serving separately, is regarded as sacrilege by purists, but it is commonplace, even so. Try other protein foods in place of the crab and ham, as in the variations listed. Use the dish as a basis of experimentation – this is a good-natured dish!

125 g cooked, shelled crab meat
125 g cooked smoked ham
125 g canned water chestnuts
8 spring onions
4 tablespoons groundnut,
sunflower or safflower oil
2 onions, chopped
750 g cooked, cool, long grain white
rice (from 500 g of raw rice)
3 free-range eggs, beaten
2 tablespoons black bean sauce
2 tablespoons fish sauce,
such as *nam pla* or *nuoc mam*
1 tablespoon sweet chilli sauce,
or garlic-chilli sauce
1 tablespoon passata or tomato juice
1 large bunch of flat leaf parsley
salt and freshly ground pepper

Variations:
Smoked Fish Fried Rice:
125 g smoked sturgeon or halibut
125 g prosciutto
1 large bunch of chives
Chicken, Smoked Seafood and
Tarragon Fried Rice:
125 g cooked chicken
125 g smoked oysters, mussels or eel
1 large bunch of tarragon
Serves 4–5

Finely slice the crab meat and smoked ham, drain and slice the water chestnuts and finely slice the spring onions diagonally, then set aside until you are ready to assemble the dish.

Heat a wok or deep-sided frying pan. Add the oil and, when hot, add the onions and fry over a medium heat until translucent. Add the crab meat and ham and cook for a further 2 minutes, uncovered, until hot.

Add the cooked rice, heat and stir, then cover and cook, undisturbed, for about 5 minutes or until heated through. Add the water chestnuts.

Season the eggs with salt and pepper and pour them into a hollow in the centre of the rice. Stir around the edges, until just beginning to set, then stir the egg from the middle to the outer edge so the egg sets quickly, but is still moist.

Add the three sauces and passata to the rice, then add the spring onions, tossing quickly into the hot rice.

To serve, scissor-snip the parsley, then scatter it over the dish. Serve hot while the egg is still creamy: the mixture will continue cooking on the plate.

Variations:

To make the Smoked Fish Fried Rice, cut the smoked sturgeon or halibut into pieces, and substitute for the crab. Slice the prosciutto and substitute for the ham. Snip the chives and use instead of the parsley. Proceed as in the main recipe, keeping the sauces the same.

The Chicken, Smoked Seafood and Tarragon Fried Rice is an excellent use for leftover roast chicken. Shred the chicken finely, then proceed as in the main recipe, substituting chicken instead of the ham, the smoked oysters, mussels or eel instead of the crab and scissor-snipped tarragon instead of the parsley. Use the same sauces as in the main recipe.

Note: White, long grain rice is traditionally used to make fried rice, and purists insist it should stay snowy white. However, I have also cooked it with brown rice, which tastes very good indeed.

Crispy fritters with interesting ingredients found in Caribbean markets, Asian grocers and larger supermarkets. Serve with two dipping sauces: a Sweet-sour dip containing 4 tablespoons rice vinegar, a little chopped spring onion and garlic, plus salt, pepper and sugar to taste. Make a Chilli-sesame dip with 4 tablespoons rice vinegar, plus chopped red and green chillies, and 2 teaspoons each of sesame seeds, sesame oil and fish sauce.

ukoy
sweet potato fritters
with plantains and prawns

250 g whole uncooked prawns
75 ml boiling water or fish stock
1 small red pepper
5 cm piece of fresh ginger
2.5 cm lemongrass or lemon zest
4 spring onions, finely sliced
175 g sweet potato
250 g ripe plantain or green banana
2 eggs
1 teaspoon turmeric
125 g rice flour
4 garlic cloves, chopped
2 teaspoons baking powder
groundnut oil, for frying
salt and freshly ground black pepper
Makes 24, serves 4–6

Shell the prawns and set the tail meat aside. Crush the shells well, put in a pan with the water or stock, and simmer, covered, for 5 minutes. Strain into a bowl, pressing through as much flavour as possible. Discard the debris and cool the stock. Deseed and core the red pepper and cut into 1 cm pieces. Peel the fresh ginger and finely slice it lengthways. Finely slice the lemongrass crossways. Cut the sweet potato into 5 mm cubes. Peel the plantain and cut into small cubes.

Meanwhile whisk the eggs and stock into the turmeric, rice flour, garlic, baking powder, salt and black pepper. Add the red pepper, ginger, lemongrass, spring onions, plantain, sweet potato and prawn tails. Mix quickly together.

Heat about 2.5 cm groundnut oil in a heavy-based frying pan or wok, to 190°C, or until 1 cm cube of bread turns golden brown in about 40 seconds.

Put 4 spoonfuls of the mixture in the hot oil and cook for 50–90 seconds on each side, turning over with tongs. Drain on crumpled kitchen paper and keep hot while you cook the remaining mixture. Serve with your choice of dipping sauces, as described in the introduction to this recipe.

Mee *krob* is the classic Thai dish that ideally requires a large wok, a pair of tongs and a ventilator fan. But care, optimism and an open window will do – and don't try to cook more than one skein of dried vermicelli noodles at a time. Buy the noodles, rice vinegar, fish sauce, *tom yam* stock cubes and tiny, fiercely hot, birds-eye chillies from an Asian grocer.

crispy thai noodles
with chicken, prawns, chilli and coriander

250 g fine rice vermicelli noodles
groundnut oil, for deep-frying
3 eggs, beaten
100–125 g caster sugar
6 tablespoons rice vinegar
4 tablespoons light soy sauce
4 tablespoons Thai fish sauce
100 ml spicy stock, such as stock made from *tom yam* stock cubes
1 tablespoon mild paprika
2 teaspoons coriander seeds, crushed
250 g uncooked prawns, shelled and deveined
4 skinless, boneless chicken breasts, finely sliced
175 g fresh bean sprouts
6 spring onions, sliced lengthways
3–4 birds-eye chillies, sliced crossways
1 bunch of fresh coriander, chopped

Serves 4–6

Separate the layered skeins of noodles without breaking them. Cook one skein at a time. Pour about 5 cm groundnut oil into a large wok and heat to 190°C, or until one strand puffs up immediately. Set a large metal sieve over a heatproof bowl. Put crumpled kitchen paper on a tray, ready for draining the fried noodles. Using tongs, add a skein of noodles to the very hot oil. Cook for 10–15 seconds until puffed up and slightly browned, then turn it over carefully with tongs. Cook the second side, then set it on the kitchen paper. Repeat until all the noodles have been cooked. If there is any dark debris in the oil, pour all the oil through the sieve into the heatproof bowl, discard the debris and return the oil to the wok. Reheat and continue cooking the remaining noodles. Pour out the hot oil, return the cooked noodles to the empty wok, and keep them warm.

Heat a small pan, add 1 tablespoon of hot oil, then half the eggs. Cook the omelette briefly on both sides. Remove and repeat with the remaining mixture. Roll up the omelettes, slice into strips and set aside.

Wipe out the pan and add the sugar, vinegar, soy and fish sauces, stock, paprika and coriander. Heat, stirring, until syrupy. Add the prawns and poach until firm. Remove and set aside. Cook the chicken in the same way. Increase the heat, add the beansprouts, spring onions, omelette and prawns, and toss gently. Tip the mixture over the hot noodles in the large wok. Turn the noodles to coat, breaking them as little as possible. Add the chillies and coriander, and serve hot.

Rice sticks are dried noodles packed in large skeins. The noodles are about 5 mm wide, and are a brilliant larder standby item – very versatile and easy to prepare. Szechuan peppercorns (*Zanthoxylum simulans*) are scented and spicy, rather than hot. They are available from Chinese food stores or specialist spice merchants.

rice sticks
with Szechuan-style sauce

150 ml groundnut oil

125 g shelled raw peanuts

2 teaspoons Szechuan peppercorns

1 small onion, chopped

2 garlic cloves, crushed

300 ml freshly made, strong, hot China tea, or green tea

2 tablespoons dark soy sauce

1–2 tablespoons dark sesame oil

5 cm fresh root ginger, peeled and finely sliced

2 teaspoons mild paprika

3–4 dried birds-eye chillies, crumbled

juice of 1 lemon

Rice Stick Salad:

250 g celery stalks

2 cooked chicken breasts

175 g mangetout peas

250 g carrots, finely sliced

6–8 green lettuce leaves

250 g dried 'rice stick' noodles

1 bunch of fresh coriander leaves, torn

Serves 4

Heat the oil in a wok to about 190°C, or until a cube of bread browns in 40 seconds. Add the peanuts and Szechuan peppercorns and cook, stirring, for 1½ minutes. Empty the pan into a metal sieve set over a heatproof bowl. (This prevents the nuts overcooking and scorching.)

Put the contents of the sieve, plus 2 tablespoons of the cooking oil, into a food processor with the onion, garlic and half the hot tea. Whizz to a paste. Add the remaining tea, soy sauce, sesame oil, ginger, paprika, chillies and lemon juice, and whizz again to make a sauce.

Remove the leaves from the celery and reserve. Pull the cooked chicken into shreds, or cut into cubes, and finely slice the mangetout, carrots, celery stalks and lettuce. Put the chicken and vegetables in a pan with some salted boiling water. Cook for 2 minutes, drain and discard the liquid.

Meanwhile, pour boiling water over the noodles and leave to 'cook' for 3–4 minutes or until white and firm. Drain. Just before serving, reheat by pouring over boiling water, then drain quickly and add to the other ingredients.

Put the rice stick noodles in a bowl, add the vegetables, chicken and sauce and toss well. Scatter with the torn coriander and celery leaves and serve.

ozoni new year soup
with grilled *mochi* rice cakes

There are many versions of this classic celebration soup, but the one constant is the use of *mochi* rice cakes – the dense, sticky, paste-cakes, which even feature in Japanese folklore. *Mochi*, like *konbu*, bonito flakes and daikon, can all be found at Japanese grocers or speciality Asian suppliers. What may be confusing is that there are two kinds available – the soft, freshly made ones, and the hard, dry, pre-packed type. It's the latter you need, which you soak for about 5–10 minutes, until softened.

Dashi (stock):

15 g *konbu* (dried kelp)

1.2 litres cold water

50 ml sake or rice wine

15 g dried bonito flakes

Ozoni:

10 cm daikon (white radish)

1 large carrot, trimmed

4 spring onions

4 sprigs edible chrysanthemum leaves (*shungiku*)

375 g boneless, skinless chicken breasts, finely sliced

6 uncooked tiger prawn tails, deveined

5 cm of fresh root ginger, finely sliced lengthways

1 teaspoon salt

2–3 tablespoons Japanese light soy sauce (*shoyu*), or more to taste

4 *mochi* cakes (Japanese dried rice cakes)

Serves 6

1 Heat the *konbu* and water to just below boiling. Remove from the heat and let stand for 5 minutes. Remove the *konbu*. Add the sake and bonito flakes and return to the boil. Simmer 2 minutes, then strain back into the pan.

2 Trim the radish as shown, and slice thinly. Make V-shaped cuts down the length of the carrot and slice thinly. Slice the spring onions lengthways. Tear the chrysanthemum leaves, blanch for 60 seconds, drain and refresh in cold water.

3 Add the chicken, prawns and ginger to the konbu stock. Simmer, covered, for 2 minutes. Add the blanched vegetables to the soup. Add salt and soy sauce, then cover with a lid and simmer gently.

4 To prepare the *mochi* rice cakes, pour near-boiling water over them and set aside for 5–10 minutes until softened. Drain, then set aside until ready to grill. Cook under a hot grill until puffed and golden. Grill the other side.

5 Put one grilled *mochi* cake at the bottom of each soup bowl, then add the soup, taking care to give each bowl a roughly equal share. Serve hot as one course of a celebratory meal.

Go to a South-east Asian or Chinese supermarket for the various authentic ingredients. Don't be put off by the list – going shopping is half the fun! Cashews, native to Brazil, came to Malaysia with the Portuguese 400 years ago, and are a great alternative if you can't find real candle nuts.

laksa
malay noodle soup

250 g dried rice sticks

250 g uncooked prawn tails

100 g bean sprouts

1 tablespoon light soy sauce

400 ml canned coconut milk

250 g ready-made fish balls

4–6 fresh langoustines (optional)

½ cucumber

1 large bunch of fresh mint

4 lettuce leaves

Rempah Seasoning:

5 cm fresh galangal or ginger

8 candle nuts, cashews or macadamias

1–2 dried red chillies

10 cm piece lemongrass

1 tablespoon coriander seeds

4 tablespoons groundnut oil

2 garlic cloves, slivered

8 shallots or 2 onions, sliced

2 teaspoons hot paprika

1 tablespoon dried shrimp paste

2 teaspoons ground turmeric

100 g dried shrimp

Serves 4–6

To make the rempah seasoning, slice the galangal or ginger, chop the cashew or candle nuts, deseed and chop the chillies, finely slice the lemongrass lengthways, and crush the coriander seeds. Heat the groundnut oil in a small pan, add all the rempah ingredients and stir-fry for 5 minutes.

To make the soup, put the rice stick noodles in a bowl, pour over boiling water, soak for 5 minutes, then drain carefully and ladle them into 6 small bowls or 1 large serving bowl.

Shell and devein the prawn tails and put in a large pan with the bean sprouts, soy, coconut milk, fish balls and langoustines, if using. Add 1 litre of boiling water and simmer for 5 minutes.

To prepare the garnishes, cut the cucumber into 5 cm batons, finely slice the lettuce and tear the mint leaves. Set aside.

Add a ladle of the boiling soup to the pan, then stir the spicy mixture back into the soup and simmer for 6–7 minutes. Put the garnishes on top of the noodles in the bowl or bowls. Reheat the pan of soup to near-boiling, stirring to prevent the coconut oil from separating. Ladle the hot broth into the bowls – this will instantly reheat the noodles. Take care to give each bowl a roughly equal share of the solids. Serve hot while all the colours, tastes and textures remain vivid.

Note: For a main course dish, double the quantity of prawns, dried shrimp and fish balls, and add an extra 500 ml of water.

These rice flour pancakes are sometimes called 'Korean pizzas' by Korean expatriates – they are snack foods often served outdoors, at markets, fairs and celebrations.
In this version I use oysters , but clams or abalone could also be included. Dip the torn or cut portions of the pancakes into the flavourful sauce before eating.
Dried Korean chilli is sold as either shreds or grains – but you could also use chilli powder or crushed chillies.

korean oyster 'pizzas'
with chilli-sesame dipping sauce

500 g fresh oysters, shucked, or about 300 g canned oysters in brine, or other seafood
125 g rice flour
125 g plain white flour
½ teaspoon salt
1 large egg
1 teaspoon dark sesame oil
8–12 spring onions
4 tablespoons groundnut oil, for frying
Chilli-sesame Dipping Sauce:
6 tablespoons Japanese soy sauce
4 tablespoons Japanese rice vinegar
2 shallots, finely sliced
1 tablespoon toasted sesame seeds
½ teaspoon chilli shreds or grains, crushed chillies or chilli powder

Serves 4

If using fresh oysters, shuck them and reserve the liquid from the shells. If using oysters in brine, drain them and reserve the brine. Make up the liquid to 250 ml with water. (If using smoked oysters in oil, discard the oil.)

Sift the flours and salt into a bowl. Whisk in the brine or oyster-water, together with the egg and sesame oil, to form a thin, creamy batter. Let stand while you prepare the other ingredients. Cut the spring onions in half crossways and slice the green parts into diagonal shreds. Cut the white parts lengthways into quarters.

To prepare the dipping sauce, briefly whizz all the ingredients in a blender. Pour into 4 serving dishes.

Heat 1 tablespoon of the oil in a heavy-based frying pan or wok, swirling it around to coat well. Toss in a quarter of the oysters and a few bits of spring onion. Add a quarter of the batter and some more of the spring onion. Cook the pancake 4–5 minutes, turn it and cook a further 3–4 minutes, until the surface is mottled with brown. Tear into 4 pieces and keep hot, while you cook the remaining pancakes, then serve with small bowls of the chilli-sesame dipping sauce.

góï cuốn
ricepaper parcels
with hot and sesame dips

A traditional Vietnamese dish served at communal meals and assembled at the table by the guests. It contains rice in two forms; as **wrappers** (*bañh trang*) and as rice vermicelli **noodles**. Both are sold dry by Asian grocers or larger supermarkets. This recipe, unusually, includes two **dipping sauces** – a spicy, dry mix and a sweet-sour sauce. Vietnamese mint isn't always available, so you could substitute ordinary garden mint or basil instead.

125 g dried rice vermicelli noodles
100 g pork fillet, thinly sliced
200 g bacon, cut in 32 pieces
32 ricepaper wrappers (*bañh trang*)
16 small uncooked prawns, shelled, deveined, and halved (about 250 g)
125 g fresh bean sprouts
16 spring onions
8 lettuce leaves, quartered
32 mint or Vietnamese mint leaves
Spicy Chilli Dipping Sauce:
2–3 red or green birds-eye chillies, finely sliced
4 tablespoons toasted sesame seeds
4 tablespoons desiccated coconut
Sweet-sour Dipping Sauce:
3 limes
3 tablespoons fish sauce (*nuoc mam*)
1 tablespoon sugar
2 teaspoons peeled, grated fresh root ginger
Makes 32, serves 6–8

1 To 'cook' the rice vermicelli noodles, put in a strainer set over a large saucepan. Cover with boiling water and leave for 5 minutes. Drain, rinse in cold water to stop the cooking process, then drain again. Set aside.

2 Place the ingredients for the Spicy Chilli Dipping Sauce in a small serving bowl and mix well. To make the Sweet-sour Sauce, finely slice the lime zest and squeeze the juice. Mix with the other ingredients in a small bowl.

3 Preheat a griller or stove-top grill pan: cook the pork and bacon on the grill pan for 2–3 minutes, or under the griller on a foil-lined rack, turning the pieces over from time to time until cooked and moist, but not crisp. Set aside.

4 Dip the ricepaper wrappers in hot water, or brush them with the water. Put on a serving platter and cover with a damp cloth. Alternatively, have the guests dip their own wrappers.

5 Pour boiling water over the prepared prawns. Let stand a few minutes. Rinse in cold water, then drain. Repeat with the bean sprouts. Cut the spring onions in half crossways, then lengthways, giving 64 pieces.

6 To assemble the rolls, put lettuce on a softened wrapper, add a share of the pork, bacon, prawns, noodles, mint, bean sprouts and spring onions. Roll up, with the spring onion leaves protruding, and serve with the dips.

nasi goreng

indonesian fried rice

with garnishes

Like Cantonese fried rice, *nasi goreng* has travelled all over the world and been adapted along the way. Some Indonesians maintain that it originated in China, but it has always been associated with the *rijsttafel* of Dutch colonial rule. It can combine cooked rice, omelette strips (in this case chilli-seasoned as well), vegetables, meat, fish and aromatics.

Cook the rice 2–3 hours ahead. When ready to prepare the fried rice, heat 1 tablespoon of the oil in a frying pan and fry the steak over high heat to seal on both sides – do not cook it fully. Let cool, cut into thin strips, and set aside.

If using dried onion flakes (not the ready-cooked ones) fry them in 1 tablespoon of the oil until crisply brown. Set aside.

Using a fork, beat the eggs with the chilli and salt. Add 1 tablespoon oil to the frying pan, pour in half the egg mixture, adding a little more oil if needed, and make a thin omelette. Turn it over and cook until pale gold on both sides. Make a second omelette with the remaining mixture. Roll up both omelettes up, slice finely and set aside.

Put the chopped onions, garlic and shrimp paste into a food processor and purée to a rough pulp. Heat 2 tablespoons of the remaining oil in a large wok or deep frying pan, add the pulp and fry for 3–4 minutes until cooked and dry.

Add the remaining 2 tablespoons of oil, the meat, prawns, cucumber, carrots and peas or beans. Stir-fry for 2 minutes, then add the rice. Mix well, then sprinkle with soy sauce. Cover and cook briefly to reheat all ingredients, sprinkling in a little water as needed to help create the necessary steam. Scatter over the spring onions and onion flakes and serve.

750 g cooked white long-grain rice

7 tablespoons groundnut oil

375 g rump steak or pork steak

4 tablespoons ready-fried onion flakes

(or dried onion flakes)

3 eggs

1 teaspoon dried crushed chilli

½ teaspoon salt

2 onions, chopped

3–4 garlic cloves, crushed or finely sliced

1 teaspoon shrimp paste (*blachan*)

250 g uncooked prawn tails, shelled and deveined

10 cm cucumber, cut into matchsticks

1 carrot, finely sliced and blanched

125 g fresh peas or beans, blanched

2 tablespoons light soy sauce

4 spring onions, finely sliced lengthways

Serves 4

japanese sushi

One of the glories of the Japanese kitchen, sushi traditionally involves much ritual, but it is possible to apply the general principles using western utensils. The essentials are Japanese short grain sushi rice and other authentic ingredients. Japanese grocers stock the rice, *konbu* (kelp), *sushi-su* (rice vinegar), *kurogoma* (black sesame seeds), *umeboshi* (pickled plums), *wasabi* (green horseradish) paste and *beni-shogu* (pickled ginger). Shown here are three sushi made with two basic methods. Keep refrigerated, then return to room temperature before serving.

425 g sushi rice, washed and drained
20 cm piece dried kelp (*konbu*)
5 tablespoons Japanese rice vinegar
2 tablespoons caster sugar
2 teaspoons sea salt
7.5 cm piece root ginger, finely sliced
3 garlic cloves, crushed
50 ml Japanese soy sauce
50 g Japanese *wasabi* paste
125 g pickled pink ginger
Onigiri-zushi (Steps 2–3):
100 g lightly cooked salmon fillet
6 pickled red plums (*umeboshi*)
1 sheet dried laver seaweed (*nori*)
Norimaki-zushi (Steps 4–6):
1 egg, beaten,
pinch of powdered saffron (optional)
1 teaspoon groundnut oil
4 sheets dried laver seaweed (*nori*)
lightly toasted over a gas flame
5 cm cucumber, cut in 8 thin wedges
¼ red pepper, sliced lengthways
4 spring onions, halved lengthways
Seafood Sushi (Steps 7–8):
6 uncooked prawn tails, blanched
6 x 5 g pieces sushi-grade salmon
50 g keta or saviar (salmon eggs)
1 teaspoon black sesame seeds
6 chives
Serves 6

1 Put the rice in a pan with the kelp and 600 ml boiling water. Simmer, covered, for 18 minutes until steam holes appear in the surface. Let stand 5 minutes. Mix the vinegar, sugar, salt, ginger and garlic, and stir into the rice.

2 Using wet hands, pinch, squeeze and pat one-third of the rice into 6 even balls. Push a hole in the centre of each. Put some salmon and plum inside. Close the rice and squeeze back into shape. Continue this process to make 5 more.

3 Scissor-cut the *nori* sheet into 12 equal squares or rectangles. Set a piece under and on top of each rice ball. Pat gently to make 6 squares. Put on a serving dish. Divide the remaining rice into 2 parts.

4 Whisk the egg, 1 tablespoon water and saffron in a bowl with a fork. Heat a frying pan, add the oil, then pour in the egg mixture. Cook both sides until set but not browned. Cool then cut in half.

5 Place 4 sheets of toasted *nori* on 4 sheets of plastic wrap (instead of the traditional bamboo mat). Add a layer of rice to each. Leave 2 plain. Add the omelette, cucumber, pepper and spring onions, as shown, to the other 2.

6 Roll up the *nori*, pulling away the plastic as you go. As each roll is complete, wrap in plastic and secure the ends with rubber bands. Cut into 2 cm slices. Remove and discard the plastic. Add the filled *norimaki* to the serving plates.

7 Remove the prawn legs and snip up the belly with scissors. Open out, snip off the shell above the tail, then press flat as shown. Tap the plain slices of sushi roll into rectangles as shown in Step 8.

8 Top the plain sushi with raw salmon, salmon eggs and prawn tails. Snip the salmon and prawn to neaten the edges. Add sesame seeds and chives to the salmon. Serve all the sushi with the soy sauce, *wasabi* and pink ginger.

Black rice, grown in Thailand, Indonesia and the Philippines, is actually a dark, garnet red. Pandanus (screwpine) leaf looks like iris and is scented and sweet, but two split vanilla pods can be used instead. If you can't find the suggested tropical fruits, use the prepared fresh seasonal scarlet berries.

black coconut rice
with red berries or tropical fruits

375 g Thai or Indonesian glutinous
'black' rice (actually deep red)
2 pandanus (screwpine) leaves, crushed
and knotted (or 2 slit vanilla pods)
250 g coconut sugar, jaggery or dark
brown soft sugar
50 g coconut powder (sachet)
400 ml canned thick coconut milk
Berries or Tropical Fruits:
a selection of fresh red berries, as
shown, or tropical fruits chosen from:
2 bananas, sliced diagonally
2 mangoes, sliced into strips
I papaya, deseeded
4 rambutans (optional)
4 fresh lychees (optional)
fresh banana leaf (optional)
sprigs of mint, to serve (optional)
icing sugar, for dusting (optional)
Serves 4

Put the rice and pandanus (screwpine) leaves (or vanilla pods) in a pan with I litre of boiling water and return to the boil. Cover, reduce the heat to low, and cook, undisturbed, for about 25 minutes, or until almost dry.

Remove from the heat and let stand for 10 minutes.

Add the sugar, coconut powder and a quarter of the coconut milk, and stir until dissolved.

Prepare the berries or bananas, mangoes and papaya. If using rambutans, cut horizontally around the fruit to expose the white flesh at the centre. Pull off and discard the top skin. If using lychees, peel and discard the skin.

To serve, if liked, wash and dry 2 squares of banana leaf and use to line a large serving dish. Overlap the leaves so the 8 points stick up at the edges. Spoon in the still-hot rice.

If not using leaves to serve, simply spoon into a serving dish, or divide the rice between 4 small plates.

Trickle over some of coconut milk, and serve the rest in a small jug. Pile the fruit on top of the rice, add a sprig of mint and dust with icing sugar, if using.

Most Australians and New Zealanders are **descended** from immigrants from Europe, South-east Asia, the Far East, the Middle East, and the Americas. Today, their delicious, modern **multi-cultural cuisines** show influences from all of these culinary forebears.

australia
and new zealand

rice and papaya salad
with banana ribbon crisps and chilli-lime dressing

Papaya and mango (shown below) are often used as vegetables in their green, unripe state. Look out for them in Asian greengrocers and even some enlightened supermarkets. Select smoked seafood with a delicate texture: smoked halibut, sturgeon or eel, hot-smoked mackerel or trout, smoked clams, mussels or even oysters all work well. Serve this salad, ideally while the rice is fresh-cooked and warm, and the garnishes cold. Choose an interesting sweetening agent for your dressing. Heap the salads up into good high piles. Be relaxed – this is bistrôt fare!

175 g white easy-cook basmati rice

1 cinnamon stick

Chilli-lime Dressing:

1 medium-hot red serrano chilli

4 limes

4 tablespoons fish sauce (*nam pla*)

25 g palm sugar, jaggery or

light soft brown sugar

Green Papaya Salad:

2 small or 1 medium sized green

(unripe) papaya or green mango

50 g fresh coriander leaves

2 tiny green birds-eye chillies

50 g fresh mint leaves

250 g smoked seafood

50 g dry-roasted peanuts, chopped

1 tablespoon pink peppercorns

(optional)

Banana Ribbon Crisps:

1 underripe, green banana, peeled

4–6 tablespoons groundnut oil

Serves 4–6

Briefly rinse and drain the rice, and put in a medium-sized pan with the cinnamon stick and a little over twice its volume (about 450 ml) of boiling water. Return to the boil, reduce the heat to very low, cover the pan and cook, undisturbed, for 15–18 minutes or until all liquid is absorbed, the rice is light and fluffy and steam holes appear on the surface. Let stand, covered, for 5 minutes. Deseed the chilli and slice finely. Finely slice the zest of 1 of the limes, and reserve. Squeeze the juice from all 4 limes, and put in a blender with the fish sauce, sugar and chilli. Whizz to a froth. Stir half the mixture through the hot rice. Remove the cinnamon stick and reserve.

To make the salad, peel the papaya or mango, and remove and discard the papaya seeds. The large mango seed must also be discarded.

Using a food processor, mandoline or coarse grater, finely slice the papaya or mango. Scissor-snip the coriander leaves, and finely slice the birds-eye chillies crossways. Put the coriander and chillies in a bowl with the mint, seafood, peanuts and pink peppercorns, if using. Toss with the remaining dressing.

To make the fried banana garnish, use a potato peeler to slice the banana lengthways into long ribbons. Heat the oil until very hot in a wok or frying pan and fry the banana ribbons until crisp and curly. Drain on kitchen paper and discard the oil.

Put a mound of dressed rice on each plate, then add the papaya salad, banana ribbons and reserved zest. Set some fragments of the cinnamon, pulled into pieces, beside the salad.

Note: If the rice must be cooked ahead, microwave it briefly or steam in a steamer until barely hot. Add its dressing and assemble remaining salad, as above.

These crusty, crunchy cakes of rice with a cheesy, sticky centre are a great treat. Add to these some succulent, char-grilled or plainly grilled fish and a quick-cook pickle of mustard seed, cucumber and sweet-sharp red chilli (almost like a jam), and you have a superb, stylish dish for lunch, supper or a party.

sticky risotto pancakes
with grilled fish and chilli pickle

1 kg cooked, chilled risotto (saffron, lemon or plain) containing at least 50 g grated Parmesan, or more
50 g polenta grain, to coat
4 tablespoons extra-virgin olive oil
Grilled Fish:
4 boneless fish fillets, such as red mullet, red snapper, gurnard or trout, about 125 g each
4 garlic cloves, crushed to a purée
sea salt and freshly ground pepper
Chilli Pickle:
6 tablespoons rice vinegar
3 tablespoons caster sugar
1 teaspoon mustard seeds
1 medium hot red chilli, deseeded and finely sliced
100 g cucumber, unpeeled, finely sliced lengthways
Serves 4

Divide the cooked risotto into 8 equal portions. Squeeze each one into a ball, then mould into 7.5 cm round cakes. Pat in polenta to cover.

If using a char-grill, large cast iron pan or non-stick frying pan, preheat it, then brush with a drizzle of oil. Set all the rice cakes in position at once, and press down towards the end of cooking time, about 7–8 minutes. Turn and cook the second side for about the same time.

If using a traditional grill, preheat first, then cover the rack with foil. Pour half the oil over the foil and put the rice cakes on top. Drizzle with the remaining oil and grill for 7–8 minutes on each side or until pleasantly crusty.

Towards the end of the cooking time prepare the fish: rub some garlic on to each skinless surface. Season well, then add to the grill pan, char-grill, or frying pan. Cook, pressing down firmly, for 2–2½ minutes each side. (If using red mullet cook for only about 1¼–1½ minutes on each side.)

If using a grill, cook until flaky, about 2–3 minutes on each side, or a little less for red mullet.

To make the pickle, combine all the ingredients in a small saucepan. Stir and boil, uncovered, until the cucumber wilts.

To serve, put the rice cakes on each plate and set the fish on top. Spoon over some pickle and its liquid and serve hot.

Note: 375 g raw risotto rice yields 1 kg cooked weight.

sesame vermicelli
noodles with aubergines and pears

An exotic but easy salad combination, concentrating on textures and exotic tastes. It borrows ingredients from various Asian-Pacific cultures but belongs specifically to no particular one, though it follows classic lines. Many books advise long-soaking noodles in cold water, but I prefer the speedy approach: these vermicelli noodles are virtually cooked by having near-boiling water poured over them.

Preheat the char-grill or grill. Cut the aubergines into quarters, lengthways, then grill them first insides up, then skin sides up, until charred, soft and aromatic – about 15 minutes altogether. Cut into 1 cm chunks and set aside.

Put the noodles, star anise and fungus in a bowl, then pour over boiling water. Let stand for 8 minutes, then drain, reserving 4 tablespoons of the liquid.

To make the dressing put this liquid in a blender with the tahini paste, coconut milk, garlic, soy sauce and half the sesame oil. Whizz until frothy. Pour over the drained noodles and toss gently to coat. Divide between 4 plates, adding an anise pod and some fungus to each one.

Slice the cucumber and nashi pears into matchstick strips. Toss the aubergine, cucumber and nashi in the remaining sesame oil and the juice of 2 of the limes, then scissor-snip the parsley and add to the bowl. Spoon the mixture over the noodles, then sprinkle with the black sesame seeds. Cut the remaining lime into wedges and add to the plates.

2 medium aubergines

175 g dried rice vermicelli noodles

8 star anise pods

about 15 g dried black Chinese fungus (8 whole or 20–30 pieces)

½ cucumber

2 nashi (Asian) pears

3 limes

1 large bunch flat leaf parsley

1 teaspoon black sesame seeds, or black onion seeds (nigella)

Tahini Dressing:

2 tablespoons tahini (roasted sesame seed) paste

150 ml thick coconut milk

4 garlic cloves, crushed

2 tablespoons light soy sauce

2 tablespoons dark sesame oil

Serves 4

Rice in a pie? The idea may seem odd, but this brasserie-style dish is fascinating. A fresh salsa is the second surprise – feijoas are green tropical fruit with a superb, scented taste. They grow well in the Antipodes and are also exported. Kiwifruit taste different, but have similar texture.

rice tart
with a feijoa salsa

150 g shortcrust pastry or *pâte brisée*, chilled
250 g white easy-cook long grain rice or basmati easy-cook rice
4 tablespoons sweet chilli sauce
1 tablespoon wasabi paste
150 ml late-picked riesling, muscatel or other sweet dessert wine
5 cm fresh ginger, finely sliced
1 teaspoon black onion seeds (nigella) (optional)

Feijoa Salsa:
4 ripe feijoas or kiwifruit
2 spring onions, finely sliced
1 red serrano chilli, sliced
2 garlic cloves, crushed
1 large bunch of fresh flat leaf parsley, scissor-snipped
2 tablespoons fish sauce (*nam pla*)
2 teaspoons vanilla sugar
2 tablespoons rice vinegar
salad leaves, to serve

Serves 6–8

Roll out the pastry very thinly and use to line a deep 20 cm flan tin, fluted or plain. Don't worry about untidy edges – they become crisp and can be broken off later. Prick the base with a fork. Line the flan case with bakewell paper and baking beans. Bake blind towards the top of a preheated oven at 200°C (400°F) Gas Mark 6 for 15 minutes. Remove the paper and baking beans and cook for a further 10 minutes or until the pastry is golden and crisp. As soon as the pastry goes into the oven, cook the rice with about twice its volume (450 ml) of boiling water for 15–18 minutes, until the water is absorbed, steam holes appear in the top and the rice is fluffy. Leave the cooked rice to stand for 5 minutes more, covered.

Dissolve the chilli sauce and wasabi paste in the wine. Add the ginger, then stir lightly through the rice. Remove the cooked pastry case from the oven and spoon in the seasoned rice – level the surface, but do not pack it heavily. Sprinkle the black onion seeds over the top if using. Let stand.

To make the salsa, cut the feijoas in half crossways and scoop out the flesh with a teaspoon into a small bowl. Discard the skins. (If using kiwi fruit, treat them the same way.) Add the spring onion, chilli, garlic, parsley, fish sauce, sugar and vinegar. Taste and adjust the seasonings. Serve warm or cool, but not chilled – on the same day as it is made – in wedges with a dollop of salsa on top and a few salad leaves.

rice varieties

White Long Grain
(Texmati, Carolina, Patna, etc.)
Long grain, white, milled, not glutinous.
Comments: Mainly savoury use. Absorbs double its volume of liquid. Useful all-purpose rice needing assertive seasoning. Favourite all-purpose and everyday rice in the West. Many varieties available. Cooks with separate grains.
Sources: Grocers, supermarkets, delicatessens.
Cooking and timing: 12–15 minutes or follow packet instructions. Cooking methods; pan-of-water, absorption, rice cooker or microwave.

White Long Grain Easy-cook Rice
(Parboiled long grain rice)
Yellowish-white (due to extra parboiling processing). Steam-treated (parboiled) then milled. Not glutinous.
Comments: Usually used in savoury dishes and as an accompaniment. All-purpose, useful, cooks with separate grains, white and fluffy. It never sticks. More nutritious, because, before milling the grain was parboiled (partially steam treated, which effectively gelatinizes some of the starch.) So more of the B-vitamins are driven deeper into the endosperm or inner part. This means it needs several minutes' extra cooking time. Purists maintain that flavour and aroma are unfavourably affected by the processing. Chefs and caterers prize it for its separate grains. (Note: Italian version is plumper and cooks in 10–12 minutes.)
Sources: Grocers, supermarkets, delicatessens, catering suppliers.
Cooking and timing: 20–25 minutes or follow packet instructions. Cooking methods; pan-of-water, absorption, rice cooker, microwave.

Brown Long Grain Rice
(American wholegrain long grain rice, Texmati, Carolina, Patna, etc.)
Long, slim grain, brown, hulled but not milled. Not glutinous.
Comments: Mainly savoury dishes and accompaniments. Absorbs 3–4 times its volume of stock or water. Bulky, filling, substantial. Average cost.
Cooks with a chewy texture, nutty flavour and is slightly less separate than white. Useful, all-purpose grain, good with distinctive seasonings and flavourings, especially garlic, fresh herbs and spices.
Sources: Grocers, supermarkets, delicatessens and wholefood stores.
Cooking and timing: 45–50 minutes or follow packet instructions. Takes longer than white rice because it is less refined. Cooking methods; pan-of-water, absorption, pressure cooker or microwave.

Brown Wholegrain Easy-cook Long Grain
(Brown easy-cook long grain rice)
Long grain, parboiled, unpearled. Golden brown (due to extra parboiling process). Steam-treated (parboiled) but not milled. Not glutinous.
Comments: Mainly savoury use. Highly nutritious but harder for some to absorb. Dense, chewy texture, some aroma and nutty taste. B-vitamins and minerals in good amounts. High in fibre, low in calories. Takes longer to cook than white and non-steam-treated equivalent. Store in a cool, dark place or refrigerate, since natural oils in bran layer can become stale and rancid. Use promptly. Often needs assertive seasoning and flavourings such as garlic, flavoured oils, fresh herbs and spices.
Sources: Wholefood stores, good supermarkets, delicatessens, specialist grocers, wholesalers.
Cooking and timing: About 45–60 minutes (because less refined), or follow packet instructions. Cooking methods; pan-of-water, absorption, pressure cooker or microwave. Chefs and caterers prize it for its separate grains.

Spanish Calasparra
(Paella rice or Bomba, Balilla Sollana)
Round to medium grain (*Redondo*, in Spanish). White, milled. Not glutinous, but cooks to a slightly sticky but dry state.
Comments: Superb, high quality, robust rice grains: delicious, firm-textured. Calasparra is grown near the Spanish town of the same name in Murcia beside the Seguro and Mundo rivers. Governed by *Denominación de Origen* regulations, it is *Categoria Extra*. Expensive, highly regarded. Best cooked in large shallow metal *paellera* pans, lidless, with two handles. If Calasparra is difficult to find, substitute Italian risotto rice.
Sources: Spanish grocers, specialist importers, delicatessens, wholefood stores.
Cooking and timing: 15–18 minutes. Paella takes longer since many ingredients and processes are being added while rice cooks and liquid evaporates from uncovered pan. Usually absorbs 3–4 times original volume of liquid. Should cook to quite dry.

Italian Risotto Rice
(*Superfino* grade; Carnaroli, Arborio, Roma, Baldo. *Fino* grade; RB 265, Razza, Vialone, Nano. *Semifino* grade; Ardizzone, Maratello, Ribe, Europa, Loto. *Commune* or lowest grade; Ordinario, Ballila)
Milled, not glutinous. Hard, but cooks to a plump, tender, but *al dente* state.
Comments: Superb large, medium to long grain. White with visible chalky lines or dots in parts. Perfect for soupy, creamy risotto. Grown in the Po Valley in Northern Italy. Rice is the staple in the north, pasta in the south. The higher the quality the more liquid it absorbs – up to 4 times its original volume. Produces a sumptuous, creamy risotto with separate grains. (Most rice types absorb only 2–3 times their own volume.)
Sources: Italian grocers, delicatessens, specialist supermarkets, wholefood stores, specialist importers.
Cooking and timing: Carnaroli and Arborio cook in 18–20 minutes but, because of the 3 or 4 stages of adding the hot liquid, the initial cooking in butter and the regular stirring to check absorption and allow liquids to evaporate, it takes 25–26 minutes in total. (Final cooking in the oven would also add time.)

Italian Pudding Rice
Roundish, short grains. White, milled. Not glutinous, but sticky and soft.
Comments: Cooked grains cling together and don't keep a definite form. Used for sweet dishes as a thickener, especially custards, moulded desserts and puddings. Mild-flavoured, often combined with dairy products such as milk, cream, butter and eggs. Inexpensive, but can be used to create surprisingly classy dishes. (Heretical fact: could actually be used for sushi if expensive Japanese sushi rice were unavailable.)
Sources: Grocers, supermarkets, corner stores, delicatessens, wholefood stores.
Cooking and timing: About 15 minutes (though recipes often allow longer to allow for evaporation of liquids, blending of flavours and, in the case of oven cooking, formation of a brown crust or 'skin'. 50 g pudding rice can thicken 600 ml of liquid. Sets to a gel when cold.

Camargue Red Rice
(Griotto rice)
Oval, medium grain. Brownish-red colour, created by a spontaneous mutation, colour visible on pericarp. Milled, not hulled. Not glutinous (but cooks slightly sticky).
Comments: Unique strain with a subtle flavour and red colour. A premium product, often grown by organic methods. Confined to the wetlands of France's Camargue region. Similar types are indigenous to West Africa (*Oryza glaberrima*), Goa in India, and some parts of the USA. Earthy taste, chewy, firm texture, good appearance. Tipped to be a future culinary 'star'.
Like wild rice, it suits assertive treatment and seasoning, such as garlic, fresh herbs and some acidity. Excellent with game, duck or goose where colour can be used to advantage. (Beware of cooking with seafood – the natural rosy pigment dyes the fish.)
Sources: Delicatessens, specialist grocers, specialist supermarkets, wholefood stores.
Cooking and timing: 45–60 minutes or follow packet instructions. Cooking methods; pan-of-water, absorption method, pressure cooker, microwave.

Black Glutinous Rice
(Black sweet rice, wild sweet rice)
Short to medium grain. Actually garnet red, not black. Milled. Red colour only in outer layer of milled grain. Glutinous. High in amylopectin. Note: glutinous rice does not contain gluten.
Comments: Rich, earthy flavour. Combines well with coconut sugar, other palm sugars, coconut milk and pandanus. Usually used in sweet dishes. Not a staple except in Laos, Vietnam, Cambodia, Thailand. Only 2% of world harvest is glutinous (sticky) rice.

Sources: Asian grocers and supermarkets, specialist delicatessens.

Cooking and timing: 25–30 minutes. (Beware: colour 'dyes' other foods present.) Cooking methods; absorption, additional liquids as needed, rice cooker or microwave.

White Basmati Rice
(Many types, including Punni, Dehra Dun, Jeera-sali, Delhi, and the golden-hued Golden Sela and Ambre Mohu)
Long, slim grain with fine, clean scent. White, milled, not glutinous: famously separate, fluffy grains.
Comments: If most people had to choose one rice, this would be it. Grows in the Himalayan foothills and considered by many to be the world's finest rice. Often aged and always treated with respect. Wonderful aroma. Mainly savoury, used especially with curries, also in pilaus, pulaos, pollos, pilafs, pullows, where separate grains are wanted. Used in some sweet dishes such as Kheer.
Sources: Indian and Pakistani grocers, good supermarkets, delicatessens, specialist grocers, wholefood stores.
Cooking and timing: 10–12 minutes, or follow packet instructions. Amazingly convenient, mostly cooked by absorption method, but also rice cooker or microwave.

White Easy-cook Basmati Rice
As above, technically white but gold tones due to parboiling (steam treatment). Parboiled, then milled. Not glutinous.
Comments: Partially steam-treated to gelatinize some of the starch and drive valuable B-vitamins deep into the grain. Nutritionally superior, but needs several minutes extra cooking time. Each grain remains separate and fluffy. Never sticks. Process first used centuries ago in India, where it forms the staple of the traditional vegetarian diet.
In the West, it is most favoured by chefs who prefer each grain to remain separate. In culinary terms it is considered to have a less superb scent and its taste is somewhat altered, making it less desirable to some people. In India, largely nutritional issues dominate in its choice and use.
Sources: Most grocers, supermarkets.
Cooking and timing: 18–20 minutes or

according to packet instructions – longer than untreated basmati. Mostly cooked by absorption method, but also by pan-of-water, rice cooker or microwave.

Brown Basmati Rice
('Unpearled' or 'unpolished')
Long, slim grain. Brown, not milled. Only husk removed. Not glutinous.
Comments: Use as basmati rice. Highly nutritious (but harder for some people to absorb). Dense, chewy texture, nutty flavour, fair aroma. High in B-vitamins and fibre but low in calories. Takes longer to cook than white basmati. Store in cool, dark place or refrigerate since natural oils in the bran can become rancid. Use promptly. Good when well-seasoned: often combined with garlic and fresh herbs.
Sources: Wholefood stores, delicatessens, good supermarkets, specialist grocers.
Cooking and timing: 45–60 minutes because it is less refined. Follow packet instructions. Cooking method; usually pan-of-water, but also pressure cooker or microwave.

Thai Fragrant Rice
(Jasmine rice, sweet rice)
Long grain. White, milled. Slightly sticky (glutinous). Note: glutinous rice does not contain gluten.
Comments: Mainly savoury use. The favourite everyday rice of Thai and South-east Asian cooks. Authentic savour for a large range of South-east Asian dishes. Slight stickiness makes it perfect for Western as well as Eastern palates. Good with Thai-style curries, stir-fries or in pulaus. Some people rinse cooked rice briefly under boiling water to separate clumps.
Sources: Asian grocers and supermarkets, specialist supermarkets, delicatessens.
Cooking and timing: 12–15 minutes, 25 if cooked in double-boiler, or follow packet instructions. Cooking methods; double boiler, absorption, pan-of-water, rice cooker or microwave.

Japanese Sushi Rice
(Japanese sweet rice, Japanese medium grain rice, Japanese sticky rice, Korean rice, Kokuho Rose)
Plump, short grain. White, milled. Glutinous.

Note: glutinous rice does not contain gluten.
Comments: Sticky, absorbent, perfect for sushi where grains must stick together. Expensive, high quality, needs less water than other types. Take care to avoid sticking.
Sources: Japanese supermarkets, delicatessens, Asian grocers, specialist supermarkets.
Cooking and timing: 15–20 minutes plus standing time, or follow packet instructions. Cooking methods; absorption, rice cooker or microwave.

Wild Rice (Zizania aquatica)
('Indian' rice, Tuscarora rice)
Very long, glossy grain. Dark brown to purplish-black, husked but not milled. Not glutinous.
Comments: Not a true rice, but an aquatic grass. Once truly wild and merely gathered in a trade mainly controlled by Native Americans. Native to Eastern, Central and North America. Now cultivated. Delicious, nutty, earthy taste works well with feathered game, poultry and wild seafood. When fully cooked it may 'flower', or 'butterfly' – one or both ends spring apart to reveal the white interior. Mainly savoury use. Expensive, good quality product. Swells to 2½–4 times original volume when cooked.
Sources: Good grocers, wholefood stores, specialist supermarkets, delicatessens.
Cooking and timing: 55–60 minutes, or follow packet instructions.

Basmati and Wild Rice Mixed
Long white (basmati) and long brown-black (wild rice) mixture. Not glutinous.
Comments: Mainly savoury use. Relatively new 'convenience' product, created in Europe, particularly useful because of speed and ease of cooking and relative cheapness (yet both are premium products). The two kinds of rice are separately pre-treated so that their eventual cooking time is equal.
Sources: Good grocers, luxury goods stores, specialist supermarkets, delicatessens, wholefood stores.
Cooking and timing: 20–25 minutes – much quicker than for traditional wild rice. Cooking methods; pan-of-water, absorption, rice cooker or microwave.

acknowledgements

My thanks go to Fiona Lindsay, Linda Shanks, Jeremy Hopley, Wei Tang , Catherine Rowlands, Fiona Smith, Annabel Hartog, Amanda Hills, Christine Boodle, and all at Ryland Peters & Small and Tilda Rice (especially Lesley Wood).

I also wish to thank the following experts and authors whose works have inspired and so informed me:
Madhur Jaffrey *The Flavours of India, Far Eastern Cookery*
Bruce Cost *Foods from the Far East*
Tess Mallos *Complete Middle Eastern Cookbook*
Charmaine Solomon *Oriental Collection*
Evan Jones *American Food: The Gastronomic Story*
Sada Fretz *Pilaf, Risotto and Other Ways with Rice*
Heidi Haughy Cusick *Soul and Spice*
Steven Raichlen *Miami Spice*
Camellia Panjabi *50 Great Curries of India*
Rena Salamon *Greek Food*
Meera Freeman *The Vietnamese Cookbook*
Claudia Roden *Mediterranean Cookery, A New Book of Middle Eastern Food*
Tom Stobart *The Cook's Encyclopedia*
Vicky Hayward *The Grain of Life, Gourmetour*
Anna del Conte *Classic Food of Northern Italy*
Elizabeth Lambert Ortiz *Japanese Cookery, The Book of Latin American Cookery*
Maria José Sevilla *Spain on a Plate*
Jean Andrews *Red Hot Peppers*
Paola Gavin *Italian Vegetarian Cookery*
Richard Olney (Ed.) *Grains Pasta and Pulses, Time Life Books*
Yamuna Devi *Art of Indian Vegetarian Cookery*
Sri Owen *The Rice Book, Indonesian and Thai Cookery*
Dorinda Hafner *A Taste of Africa*
Leslie Forbes *Recipes from the Indian Spice Trail*
John Spayde *Japanese Cookery*
Cheong Liew and Elizabeth Ho *My Food*
Susanna Foo *Chinese Cuisine*
Robert Carrier *Taste of Morocco*
Christopher Idone *Brazil: A Cook's Tour*
Francis Bissell *Sainsbury's Book of Food*
Victoria Alexander and Genevieve Harris *The Bathers Pavilion*

planning rice menus

Soups

Caldo verde soup *(Portugal)* **38**

Pumpkin chowder with rice and thyme *(France)* **41**

Ozoni New Year soup with mochi rice cakes *(Japan)* **110**

Laksa Malay noodle soup *(Malaysia)* **115**

Starters

Red mullet tamales with tomato chilli dip *(Mexico)* **18**

Suppli cheese balls with basil and pine nuts *(Italy)* **37**

Rice and buckwheat blini *(Russia)* **42**

Greek dolmathes *(Greece)* **45**

Korean oyster 'pizzas' with chilli-sesame dipping sauce *(Korea)* **116**

Ricepaper parcels with hot and sesame dips *(Vietnam)* **118**

Japanese sushi *(Japan)* **124**

Rice and papaya salad with banana ribbon crisps and
chilli-lime dressing *(Australia)* **132**

Rice tart with a feijoa salsa *(New Zealand)* **139**

Risotto, Noodles and Fried Rice

Lobster and lemon risotto on a bed of bitter greens *(USA)* **14**

Saffron risotto *(Italy)* **51**

Wild mushroom risotto *(Italy)* **51**

Classic Cantonese fried rice with spring onions, ham and crab *(China)* **102**

Fried rice with smoked fish *(China)* **102**

Fried rice with chicken, smoked seafood and tarragon *(China)* **102**

Crispy Thai noodles with chicken, prawns, chilli and coriander *(Thailand)* **106**

Rice sticks with Szechuan-style sauce *(China)* **109**

Nasi goreng Indonesian fried rice with garnishes *(Indonesia)* **122**

Sesame vermicelli noodles with aubergines and pears *(New Zealand)* **136**

Fish and Seafood

Pan-fried crab cakes with spicy oriental sauce *(USA)* **16**

Traditional jambalaya with chorizo and prawns *(USA)* **22**

Seared swordfish with wild rice and black bean salsa *(USA)* **29**

Kedgeree with smoked fish and crème fraîche *(Great Britain)* **36**

Spanish paella with chicken, prawns and squid *(Spain)* **46**

Tanzanian fish curry with mustard seed rice *(Tanzania)* **76**

Sticky risotto pancakes with grilled fish and chilli pickle *(Australia)* **135**

Poultry

Cajun gumbo with Jerusalem artichokes *(USA)* **24**

Spicy Camargue rice with char-grilled duck breasts *(France)* **52**

Chestnut rice stuffing with roasted turkey breast *(Greece)* **55**

Chicken pulau with almonds, orange and pistachio *(Afghanistan)* **64**

Chicken and peanut stew with red dendé rice *(Mali)* **77**

Chicken korma with pistachio basmati rice *(India)* **86**

Meat

Rice and peas with Jamaican hot chilli sauce *(Jamaica)* **30**

Lamb and rice sausage with parsley, lime and spices *(Iran)* **66**

Lamb biryani with coriander and cinnamon *(India)* **88**

Gingered pork chop masala with cashew rice *(India)* **92**

Vegetables

Stuffed cabbage leaves with sauerkraut and a red
pepper sauce *(Germany)* **56**

Pearl divers rice with saffron and honey *(Bahrain)* **65**

Stuffed vegetables with rice and sour cherries *(Iran)* **68**

Moroccan couscous with rice, lemon and tahini *(Morocco)* **78**

Orange and pumpkin pulao with two cachumbers and a raita *(India)* **82**

Spicy seeded pilaf with okra and spinach *(India)* **85**

Sweet potato fritters with plantains and prawns *(Philippines)* **105**

Puddings

Honey rice ice cream with orange and saffron *(Great Britain)* **61**

Almond rice custard with berries or pomegranate seeds *(Turkey)* **73**

Kheer rice pudding with cardamom and pine nuts *(Sri Lanka)* **95**

Black coconut rice with red berries or tropical fruits *(Indonesia)* **129**

Cakes and Biscuits

Spiced shortbread biscuits with rosewater and pistachios *(India)* **96**

Spicy coconut loaf with cashew nuts and cardamom *(India)* **98**

index